Better with Buttermilk

Better with Buttermilk

The Secret Ingredient in Old-Fashioned Cooking

Lee Edwards Benning

Henry Holt and Company ◆ New York

Henry Holt and Company, Inc.
Publishers since 1866
115 West 18th Street
New York, New York 10011

Henry Holt® is a registered
trademark of Henry Holt and Company, Inc.

Published in Canada by Fitzhenry & Whiteside Ltd.,
195 Allstate Parkway, Markham, Ontario L3R 4T8.

Library of Congress Cataloging-in-Publication Data
Benning, Lee Edwards.
Better with buttermilk / Lee Edwards Benning.—1st ed.
p.   cm.
Includes index.
1. Cookery (Sour cream and milk).   2. Buttermilk.   I. Title.
TX759.5.S68B46   1996
641.6'724—dc20   95-24965
                                                        CIP

ISBN 0-8050-3118-9

Henry Holt books are available for special
promotions and premiums. For details contact:
Director, Special Markets.

First Edition—1996

Designed by Paula R. Szafranski

Printed in the United States of America
All first editions are printed on acid-free paper. ∞

10   9   8   7   6   5   4   3   2   1

TO THOSE FELLOW FATHERS-IN-LAW . . .

BERNARD G. OYER,

the tester,

and

ARTHUR E. BENNING, SR.,

the taster

Contents

Preface

BUTTERMILK DEFINED

You must have seen it. Sitting there, generally right at eye level, in the refrigerated dairy case at your supermarket. But you have probably ignored it. That's the fate of buttermilk: to be overlooked. Misunderstood. Underappreciated. Which is all wrong and totally unfair.

Buttermilk has all the goodness of milk without the fat, the calories, the cholesterol.

Although called "buttermilk" from time immemorial, that's a misnomer. Buttermilk contains no butter. If anything, the more accurate description of buttermilk is butterless milk.

Traditionally, full-fat milk straight from the cow was cooled, aged, and churned. When the butter formed and was removed, the liquid left was buttermilk in the making. Omnipresent bacteria cultured the milk and turned the lactose sugar into lactic acid.

Today, some buttermilks are made essentially the same way. Others are specially cultured skim or low-fat milk. But whatever they are and however they're made, dishes are better with buttermilk.

7

Acknowledgments

A GREAT CAST OF CHARACTERS BUT NO PLOT . . .

That was how one wit described a telephone directory. It is also usually applicable to the acknowledgment pages of any nonfiction book. Usually I name the names. This time, however, I am undone. Thirty years of recipe collecting have gone into this book. And frankly I don't always know who gave me what . . . in other cases, I can't put last names to first names nor faces to names. So in a few cases, recipes will carry the source's name, but for all the many unacknowledged ones, I give leave to anyone who recognizes her or his own recipe to add a karat before the title and insert their name and accept my thanks.

Other thank yous are due to Beth Crossman, whose editing made *Better with Buttermilk* even better! And Jane Jordan Browne, my literary agent, who believed from the beginning that buttemilk was better.

Better with Buttermilk

1 Memories of Milk and Buttermilk

Oh, Fudge! Buttermilk Fudge

Chocolate Buttermilk Fudge

I was born and raised a city girl. Milk mysteriously appeared, nicely bottled, on the front step, delivered by a milkman we never saw but whose clinking bottles we heard. Buttermilk? I never heard of it until I married. My husband's drinking buttermilk was one of those little secrets husbands and wives discover about each other after marriage.

In fact, before his courtship, the closest I ever came to a cow was driving past it. Then he took me to visit his farmer brother, but only after I'd memorized all the different breeds of cows and the differences in the butterfat content of their milk. My husband was raised on a dairy farm; he knows his milk and buttermilk. In fact, his memories of the dairy barn are still fresh and vivid: "Growing up, manhood was measured by your prowess on the milking stool. Getting the milk into the bucket was not the first challenge. Nor contending with a wet, flailing tail or a stomping foot that threatened to kick the bucket. If your hands were too cold, your grip too tight, no amount of squeezing and tugging would force a reluctant cow to let down her milk. She had to be comfortable with you.

"One knew one was a milker when the cats acknowledged it. Coming to the barn in the darkness of a wintery morning, they would be waiting. A litter of kittens lined up expectantly waiting to be sprayed in the faces with warm milk straight from the cow's teat.

"From a distance of three or four feet, you would direct the stream, with some force, at the wide-open mouths . . . but at first mostly hitting eyes, nose, and ears. Still, the tiny creatures would stand their ground, later cleaning their faces by rubbing their paws on their faces and then licking them. Eventually, if one milked for enough years, one could get expert enough to bull's-eye in on one particular kitty at a time.

"Unfortunately, the milking machine made an end to that memory.

"As for buttermilk . . . we were mere preteens the day we talked Mother into letting technology take over the butter churning. I can't remember why or how we convinced her to let us sterilize the clothes washer and make the butter in there. But we did and it did. But somehow the buttermilk didn't taste the same. Cleaning up that washing machine after? That is a memory I'll never forget!

"And so back we went to the old way.

"The half-hour or so of arm-wearying cranking is over . . . the golden yellow globs of butter are removed from the wooden churn and worked or 'washed' with cold water using a wooden paddle in a wooden bowl. Finally, your cup dips into that heavenly white residue sprinkled with flecks of butter, and you quaff it down, ending with a satisfying a-a-h-h-h!

"Now, that was buttermilk!!"

I have to take him at his word. I am one of the many who suppress a shudder at the very notion of drinking buttermilk. As far as I'm concerned, the only thing worse than drinking buttermilk is cleaning the stuff out of the glass afterward.

However, in thirty some years of marriage, we have never been without a bottle of buttermilk in the refrigerator. I learned early that the way to this man's heart is through the lips, over the tongue, watch out stomach, buttermilk comes!

So, out of necessity and an excess of buttermilk, I became an expert on cooking with buttermilk. Never did I dream, however, that one single recipe would change my life. My husband does not, as a rule, read the food section of the newspaper. One day he happened to, and he found a recipe for buttermilk fudge that he wanted to try. That recipe was—to put it mildly—vague! To make a long story short, thanks to it, I became a self-taught expert on candy making and the author of my first cookbook. Here is my now-famous no-fail buttermilk fudge recipe. (If you'd like to read the entire story, you'll find it in *Oh, Fudge! A Celebration of America's Favorite Candy*, Henry Holt.)

Oh, Fudge! Buttermilk Fudge

This ten-step method produces a fudge that rivals the best that the fudge stores can produce—adapt it to any of your own recipes. This particular one is smooth, creamy, a trifle butterscotchy with a hint of something—a tang, a tartness, a je ne sais quoi *people will notice but can't identify.*

2 cups granulated sugar

1 cup buttermilk

¼ pound (1 stick) butter

1 tablespoon light corn syrup

1 teaspoon baking soda

1 teaspoon vanilla extract

1 cup coarsely chopped walnuts (optional)

Prewarm the thermometer, Measure all the ingredients (except the vanilla and nuts) and place in a 6-quart saucepan. Butter the upper sides of the saucepan. Grease and, if necessary, line a 5-by-10-inch pan. Fill a glass with ice cubes and water and fill the sink with ½ inch of cold water.

Dissolve the sugar, stirring constantly with a wooden spoon over low heat until the butter melts, the gritty sounds cease, and a spoon glides smoothly over the bottom of the pan. Increase the heat to medium and bring to a boil.

With a pastry brush dipped in hot water in a thermometer bath, wash down any crystals that may have formed; use as little water as possible. Introduce the prewarmed thermometer. Reduce the heat while retaining the boil. Stir as little as possible. Watch carefully—the mixture will really swell up. Cook until the mixture thickens.

Test in ice-cold water when the mixture thickens and the bubbles become noisy. A ball, formed in ice water, should be al dente (slightly chewy) and should hold its shape until heat from your hand begins to flatten it. Because of the acid in buttermilk, it will ball at a comparatively high temperature, approximately 238–242° F.

Shock the mixture by placing the saucepan in the sink.

Add vanilla without stirring. Allow to cool.

Stir when lukewarm and a "skin" forms on top (110° F). Return the thermometer to its water bath. Stir fudge thoroughly but not vigorously—either by hand, with an electric mixer, or food processor. Pause frequently to allow the fudge to react.

Watch for the fudge to thicken, lose its sheen, become lighter in color or streaked with lighter shades, give off some heat, or suddenly stiffen. If stirring by hand, fudge will "snap" with each stroke; by mixer, mixer waves will become very distinct; by food processor, fudge will flow sluggishly back to the center when the processor stops.

Add nuts if you wish before the fudge candies completely.

Pour, score, and store the fudge when cool in an airtight container in the refrigerator or at room temperature. This recipe can be doubled if you have a large saucepan.

Yield: 1 pound

CHOCOLATE BUTTERMILK FUDGE

To the sugar-buttermilk mixture, add 2 squares (ounces) of unsweetened chocolate broken into small pieces.

2 | Why Buttermilk Is Good for You

If there is one food that deserves to be called Nature's Own Perfected, it must surely be milk. Yet man has never been content to leave well enough alone. And to that continual quest for the new and different, we are indebted for all the many varieties of cheese, for butter, for fermented foods like yogurt, for ice creams and more. And when we could think of no new variations on milk, we looked to change milk itself.

Some of our tinkering has been beneficial; pasteurization has virtually wiped out undulant fever . . . enzyme technology has made milk more digestible for allergics . . . vitamin enrichment has improved our diet . . . and low-fat versions have probably kept a zillion arteries unclogged.

But for all the technological advances, there is a downside that Columbus couldn't have envisioned when he brought cattle to the New World on his second westward voyage in 1494.

Though few, if any, food producers will admit it, today's dairy products just aren't as delicious as they were a few decades ago. They last longer, yes, and we have many more choices than we did then. But that variety and convenience have come at the expense of taste.

Take buttermilk, for example. Made on the farm the old-fashioned way, the taste is a singular combination of sweet and tart. But when technology enabled the dairy industry to make buttermilk from skim or low-fat milk, the flavor was changed—tamed! No longer is it yesterday's rich, pleasingly tangy liquid; today, it is rather bland, something on the order of diluted yogurt. Not a change for the better according to old-timers, but yogurt lovers disagree. Cooks know that old-fashioned or modernized buttermilk remains a recipe's—and a diet's—best friend.

Think of it this way: Buttermilk is Nature's most perfect food—*with almost all of the fat removed.* Where did the fat go? Into the butter, of course.

By the way, it is technically inaccurate to speak of the *butterfat* content of milk. The correct terminology is *milk fat content.* And truly whole milk is not that 4 percent liquid sold in the dairy case; whole milk is "full-fat milk," meaning that no amount of cream has been removed.

But if there is no butter in buttermilk, why is it called *butter*milk? Because it is the milk left after the cream has been churned to remove the butter.

You might even ask, "Doesn't all the goodness leave with the butter?" And the answer is a resounding "No!" What's left, after the butter is removed, are all the milk solids, minerals, fatty acids, protein, ash—all beneficial. In fact, buttermilk is better for you in a dozen different ways:

◆ Buttermilk is low in calories, especially when made from skim or low-fat milk. It contains 88 to 120 calories per cup, compared to 149 to 159 for whole milk. Yogurt contains 50 to 100 percent more calories than buttermilk.*

◆ Buttermilk is rich in complex carbohydrates, the body's preferred energy source. Complex carbohydrates are vital for mental health because the brain is the body's only organ that cannot use glucose metabolized from protein or fat. Ounce for ounce, buttermilk contains more carbohydrates than comparable amounts of whole or 4 percent milk.

◆ Buttermilk is high in calcium. Calcium, that essential element needed to stave off the effects of bone degeneration and osteoporosis, is more abundant in buttermilk than in whole milk—295 grams average vs. 288 grams. A cup of buttermilk can supply 36 percent of the recommended daily requirement for adults.

◆ Buttermilk is also high in minerals such as phosphorous, magnesium, and potassium but, like every other dairy product, is not a very good source of iron.

◆ Buttermilk is low in cholesterol. Buttermilk from skim or low-fat milk has 10 mg cholesterol per cup, or only one-third the cholesterol of whole milk—the same or less than yogurt, and 55 percent of the cholesterol in 2 percent uncreamed cottage cheese.

◆ Buttermilk is high in essential amino acids. As mammals, our bodies are primarily protein, and protein is made up of twenty amino acids, eight of which are essential (the body synthesizes the rest). Buttermilk can supply all eight, which is more

*Unless otherwise specified, nutritional information comes from *Food Values of Portions Commonly Used,* 13th edition, by Pennington and Church, based on data collected from various sources such as the USDA and National Academy of Sciences.

than whole grain can claim. Compared to whole milk, buttermilk is higher in five of the essential amino acids, identical in one, and slightly lower in two. Bran muffins, often touted as cholesterol reducers, contain incomplete protein unless made with buttermilk.

◆ Buttermilk is vitamin rich. There's more riboflavin and thiamine in buttermilk than in whole milk, while niacin and ascorbic acid (Vitamin C) are present in about the same amounts. A good buttermilk will be fortified with Vitamins A and D—check the label. Many commercial ones aren't.

◆ Buttermilk is more easily digested than either whole or skim milk. That's because the clabbering process modifies the casein so that it is more soluble. This is good news for those who are lactose intolerant. And when used in cooking, most allergics can tolerate it, which is good news for cooks. By the way, buttermilk is just as digestible as yogurt, which has been touted for years as being easy on delicate stomachs. And it is far less expensive. For example, 8 ounces of plain yogurt costs 89 cents in my supermarket; 32 ounces of buttermilk costs 79 cents! Quite a savings!

◆ Buttermilk is tart, not sour. The tartness (slight acidification) of buttermilk counteracts sweetness in many desserts, making them subtle, not sickeningly sweet. Delicately flavored vegetables are enhanced, not overwhelmed, by buttermilk.

◆ Buttermilk is cream-thick but not as rich. As a thickener for stocks, sauces, soups, and dressings, buttermilk is a favorite of famous chefs and amateur cooks alike. Unlike cream, it thickens while reducing the caloric content. Mollie Katzen, of vegetarian cooking fame, automatically finishes every bowl of cream soup at her Moosewood restaurant by adding a dollop of buttermilk.

◆ Buttermilk is versatile. In *The New York Times Food Encyclopedia*, Craig Claiborne endorses buttermilk and its use wholeheartedly. "There are many ways—most of them not so well known"—for using buttermilk.

◆ Buttermilk is the baker's friend. Lactic acid in buttermilk gives baked goods a tenderness that they otherwise wouldn't exhibit. Cakes, pies, muffins, biscuits, and breads will keep fresh longer because of the buttermilk you substitute for whole, low-fat, or skim milk.

But don't take my word for it.

Check out any cookbook from the American Heart Association and notice the frequency with which buttermilk is specified in its recipes.

Robert E. Kowalski, the cholesterol guru, repeatedly recommends buttermilk in his two million-selling books, *8-Week Cholesterol Cure* and *8-Week Cholesterol Cure Cookbook*. As do Dr. Ron Goor and Nancy Goor in *Eater's Choice*.

Eventually some sharp Madison Avenue types will develop clever slogans to promote buttermilk as the healthiest of liquids. But you already know . . .

everything and anything
is better with buttermilk!

3 | *History of Buttermilk*

In the beginning, there was milk. Even before there was the Word, there was milk: goat's milk, camel's milk, reindeer milk, sheep's milk, yak's milk, mare's milk, mother's milk—and the most fruitful of them all, cow's milk. Interestingly, all of these milks have essentially the same composition, but they differ in proportions of fat to protein to carbohydrate, and so on.

The earliest known depiction of milking is a mosaic from Mesopotamia that shows a cow being milked, goat style, from the rear—a dangerous position if your hands are cold or you squeeze too hard, as any farmer can tell you. Milk arrives from the udder in Nature's own form of homogenization, with cream integrated into the milk. If the milk stands long enough, gravity causes the cream to rise to the top of the milk, separating the milk into the curds (cream) and whey (skim milk) of Little Miss Muffet. The skim milk is now poured off, and attention is turned to the cream. If one agitates or churns the cream, it will further separate into a fat and a liquid: butter and buttermilk. Of the three basic products we end up with—butter, buttermilk, and skim milk—the most valuable to man was the former, the least the latter. This relationship remained constant for more than four thousand years, or until modern technology began to look upon skim milk as a new profit center. Now we have skim-milk cheese and skim-milk buttermilk and, most important, nonfat dried milk, which is the same thing as skim milk.

Thus, the history of butter is in large part the history of buttermilk and of skim milk. Unfortunately, more has been written about butter than about buttermilk and skim milk.

The Hindu Vedas, sacred songs of the dwellers of India circa 1400 B.C., were the first to speak of butter making. The process has not changed much over succeeding centuries. Interestingly enough, in those days, butter was seldom eaten when first made. The general practice was to store it away after having melted it to purify it—the earliest form of ghee, or clarified butter. Butter was not considered a spread or general cooking agent but a rare flavoring agent to enhance and enrich other foods.

Without refrigeration, people had no choice but to either throw away butter when it grew rancid or to develop a taste for rancid butter. They developed a taste for it. Until the twentieth century, rancid butter in the Near and Far East was prized as an appetizer. In Dardistan, peasants relished the taste of well-aged butter. Like fine wine, aging the butter increased its value, if not its appearance (which eventually made "Louisiana blackened" look pale). In some Old World countries, hundred-year-old butter was the ultimate gourmet treat.

It should be noted that in Europe, the Irish took to burying butter in bogs to cause it to rot under semi-controlled conditions. Bog butter, buried and packed in firkins, dates back to the 1600s. Discoveries of well-aged bog butter have been found over the centuries in counties Galloway, Leitrum, and Tyrone. In *Hubredas*, a much-quoted, mock heroic poem, which satirizes the hypocrisy, churlishness, greed, pride, and casuistry of everyone, Samuel Butler (1612–1680) wrote:

> Butter to eat with their hog
> Was seven years buried in a bog.

(Buried butters have also been discovered in Iceland and Finland, where the intent may have been to "ice" and thus preserve the butter rather than "rot" it.)

A mere century ago, in areas of Asia, an individual's wealth was measured by how much butter he had stored away. According to an article published by the U.S. Department of Agriculture in 1904, the wealthiest citizens converted their other assets into butter, which they buried in the ground. Often they planted trees over the caches to ensure that these were not disturbed. When finally retrieved, the butter was deep red in color, high smelling, and highly prized.

Throughout the centuries, butter's use as a foodstuff has been minuscule because of its rarity. In the early days cows gave little milk compared to what they are bred to produce now. Being uncommon, butter was valued for its medicinal, ceremonial, and economic values. In the Grihyasutras—rules of the domestic customs and rituals of eighth- and ninth-century B.C. Hindus—appear references to bridal feasts consisting solely of milk, honey, and butter. For the wealthiest families, the ritual included taking some of the precious butter to grease the axles of the wedding carriage.

The idea of milk and honey and butter being the epitome of the feast is echoed in the Old Testament, in which Canaan is described as a "land flowing with milk and honey." Judges IV:19 tells us how the Hebrews kept their milk in animal skins, in which it soured and curdled. The curds formed a semisoft version of butter; the liquid left was a form of buttermilk.

The Romans used butter as an ointment to enrich the skin and as a dressing for the hair. We know that the Macedonians also anointed themselves with "milk oil," or butter. And the Greeks, Romans, and Scythians used butter to treat skin injuries. There is a recipe in an early medical treatise that describes how to make a salve of butter to treat wounded elephants. A soot made from burned butter was also thought to cure sore eyes.

Butter, which food historian Reay Tannahill believes originated in the cold climates of northern Europe, became a major export for Scandinavia by the twelveth century. Germany, at one point, was exporting most of its wine production to Norway in trade for butter and dried fish. However, the effect on the Norwegian people of this influx of large amounts of wine soon convinced the king of Norway to put a stop to it.

Up until the fifteenth century, milk and butter were totally foreign to the American continent. As mentioned earlier, we have Columbus to thank for introducing cows to the New World. Even so, goats proved more desirable than cattle until settlers discovered Elsie could pull wagons and plows better than Nanny or Billy. Apparently, it didn't hurt that cows also provided more meat for human consumption as well as more leather for clothing and other uses.

The milking and making of butter and cheese, as always, fell to the farm women in colonial America. The cows were milked in the pasture or field. Most of the milk production came during months when there was foraging for the stock. As a result, every housewife attempted to make enough butter during the summer to hold over through the winter.

From *The Farm Cook and Rule Book* by Nell Nichols (1924):

> Before the grass is gone in the fall and while cream is plentiful, butter may be put down for winter use. Work the butter as for immediate use, making certain that all the buttermilk is removed. Pack the butter in earthenware jars to within 5 inches of the top. Make a brine from coarse salt and water strong enough that an egg will float in it. Strain through fine cloth and pour over the butter, filling the jar. Cover the jar tightly and set in a cave or cellar. This butter will keep through the winter.

Not until the silo was invented in the late 1800s to store feed for cattle did winter milk production become a major factor. Even then, the making of butter and cheese was the most common use of milk, with milk for cooking the next. Least common was milk for drinking. Unlike today, receipts (as recipes were called) specified milk, sweet milk, and/or buttermilk; everybody knew milk meant "sour milk." The use of sweet milk was reserved for extra-special dishes, and precious buttermilk was saved for baking.

After the Civil War, the practice of driving cows and goats from house to house and milking directly into a housewife's container became popular. This practice led to door-to-door delivery of milk, butter, cheese, and eggs, which continued until the mid-1900s. Better, faster transportation and the proliferation of modern markets eventually caused the practice to virtually disappear—only to enjoy at least a temporary resurgence in some parts of the country in the 1990s.

Keeping milk "sweet" while waiting for the cream to rise to top (which took up to three days) became a challenge for post–Civil War farmers who were beginning to see dairy products as a major source of income. Some built milk houses directly over springs or wells to utilize their cooling effects.

Twice a day, fresh milk would be lugged to the milk house and poured into earthenware cream crocks, also known as Dutch potteries. Glazed inside but not outside, the crocks were wider at the top to facilitate skimming the cream. It was then stored in stone crocks to "ripen" until there was enough cream to fill the churn.

This methodology soon gave way to the use of wide pans, which were only a few inches deep. The cream separation was thus speeded up and the cream was easier to skim. And sure enough, some Swedish dairymen soon invented the "deep can" method, whereby milk was placed in tall cans and submerged in cool-temperature water. While it took a little longer for the cream to rise, more butterfat was recovered. Because the cooler temperatures kept the milk "sweeter," the resulting butter did not need to be as heavily salted. In the 1870s, Swedish butter commanded the premium price of one dollar per pound when ordinary butter was going for twenty cents—and this was back in the days when a dollar went a long way.

Thus, it became an economic duty for a housewife to keep that butter from getting rancid, and if it did, to know how to sweeten it:

> Soak the butter in water to which a small handful of baking soda has been added. After soaking some little time, drain off the water, and wash the butter with sweet milk. Work the milk out thoroughly, and the flavor of the butter will be fresh.

The next phase in butter making was the rise of local creameries in the 1870s. Most were co-ops, which benefited the farmers by not only making the butter but also selling it. Farmers delivered their milk daily and picked up their skimmed and buttermilk from the previous visit. They took the skimmed milk back to the farm to feed to pigs, calves, goats, cats, and poultry; it did a great job of fattening all of them. The buttermilk was reserved for cooking and as a beverage for children, though milk as a beverage for people remained far less in vogue than it is today.

Along came Carl Gustav Patrik de Laval and his invention, the cream separator. Creameries now had a faster, better means of getting the cream from the milk and even made their own butter and cheese. But farmers still hauled in the whole milk and hauled out the skim milk to feed to their stock and were still instructed by housewives not to forget the buttermilk if fresh rolls were wanted on the table.

In 1890, de Laval came out with what he called "Baby No. 1," a hand cream separator small enough and inexpensive enough that well-off farmers could begin separating their own cream. This they now took to the creamery only once or twice a week. The creameries were able to do without as much bulky separator space and went even deeper into butter and cheese making. At home, the hand separator made butter and cheese making less onerous, except for the children who were still pressed into service to hand-crank churns of many different kinds.

The three most common were the dasher churn, an upright churn with a plunger/dasher that is inserted in a hole in the lid; a crank churn much like an old-fashioned ice-cream machine with paddles inside; and a barrel churn that rotated back and forth something like a pendulum and could be dog- or horse-powered if there weren't a young boy about.

As cities grew, and with them the demand for milk, technology again came forward to put the creameries in a position to use virtually all of the milk for various products. To make sure they got all the whole milk they needed from the farmer on a regular basis, the creameries began picking up each day's milk at individual farms and bringing it to the creameries—first in milk cans stacked on trucks and later in shiny stainless-steel tankers.

A milk seller in Brooklyn is credited with starting the revolution in milk delivery in 1878. He put his milk up in sparkling clean glass bottles with cardboard caps—and captured the fancy of America's housewives. The trend quickly spread across the country. As late as the early 1900s, patents were still being issued for milk bottle designs.

And as always as went the history of butter, so too went the history of buttermilk. Unfortunately, since the possession of buttermilk did not signify wealth per se, we have less historical evidence for its use. We do know that buttermilk was rarely used for drinking, except among the Vikings who served it only to honored guests.

Otherwise, it too had mystical, medicinal, and practical uses. Unlike butter, which was sanctioned by religious authorities, buttermilk became part of the satanic ritual and was used in salves that supposedly made the wearer invisible, rendered him immune to pain, and enabled him to soar through the sky—or so testimony at witch trials would lead us to believe.

It also had a long history of being beauty's friend. Remember those fabled milk baths of old? Immersions in buttermilk. And they worked. Since churning at the time was less effective than now, it did not remove all the butterfat; the remaining fat softened the skin while the acid in the milk served as a natural astringent and tightened pores. In fact, into the twentieth century, buttermilk was being used by women as a do-it-yourself hand cream.

This recipe is a combination of one given to me by a friend's mother and a recipe from *Magic: An Occult Primer* by David Conway (Aquarian Press, 1988):

> Pick a handful of elderflowers *(Sambucus nigra)* and as many marigolds *(Calendula officinalis)*, a few geranium leaves. Add these plus a garlic clove to a cup of buttermilk and slowly bring it to a simmer. Cook at just the slightest tremor of a simmer for 40 minutes, then remove from the heat and let stand and steep for five hours. Reheat and melt an ounce of honey to it. Cool once more. When cold, this is guaranteed to be a "first-class restorative for jaded complexions."

Another more common use of buttermilk was for the laundry. Throughout medieval times, buttermilk was used to bleach linens. In this country during colonial days, it was greatly favored for its gentleness in bleaching skeins of linen thread:

> Lay in warm water for four days, the water being frequently changed, and the skeins wrung out. Wash them in a brook until the water comes from them clear and pure. Then buck [bleach] them with buttermilk in a bucking-tub, over and over again, then laid in clear water another week, and afterwards, seethe, rinse, beat, wash, dry and wind on bobbins.

Back in pre–Revolutionary War days, buttermilk was also treasured as a silver polish. The currency then wasn't paper but Spanish silver pieces-of-eight. When someone collected enough coins, rather than hoarding them, they were taken to a silversmith and made into a silver utensil, which was much more readily identifiable—in case of theft—than common silver coins.

The value of the utensil was essentially its weight in silver without much value being put on beauty, design, or usefulness. It therefore behooved the homemaker to polish silver as gently as possible without rubbing any off.

Salt and lemon were not used as they were on copper because this combination was too abrasive. Buttermilk was the polish of choice, as you can see from the advice of Alice Morse Earle in *Home Life in Colonial Days* (1898):

> Use full-strength [can't get] buttermilk which has been fully cultured and matured [even more impossible to get] and submerge silver until clean. Wash and dry with as little rubbing as possible.

Although today's buttermilk won't tackle tough tarnish, if used on a regular basis so that tarnish never gets a foothold, buttermilk will help retain your silver's polish.

Other uses for buttermilk were to remove freckles and as a remedy for acne. It could also be used to lighten skin to a fashionably pale tone:

> Select a medium-sized horseradish root and grate very fine. Cover with fresh buttermilk and let stand overnight. Strain through fine muslin and bottle the liquid. Wash the face with this night and morning for a bleach.

Speaking of bleach, in the days before peroxide, women were known to "condition" or thicken their hair by applying buttermilk without rinsing it out. If that should by some chance lighten it, so much the better.

Also like hydrogen peroxide, buttermilk had its uses as a medicine, for a cloth dipped in buttermilk served as a poultice for wounds. Any medicinal value came from the natural bacterial cultures. Furthermore, patients felt the lactic acid stinging and attributed it to the buttermilk's working. In a variation of the placebo effect, they were cured. Equally frequent but totally inexplicable were the headache cures attained by the use of a similar poultice.

One thing that can be said for buttermilk as a medicine is that it did no harm. And in the case of the lactose intolerant, it really does good as a stomach settler, for the conversion of lactose to lactic acid makes buttermilk more digestible than milk.

However, in 1874, buttermilk saw a new resurgence in popularity as a drink when a paper was read before the French Academe, equating buttermilk with long life à la Metchnikoff's yogurt longevity theory a century later. According to the *Valley Farmer* of Windsor, Vermont (February 21, 1874), M. Robin said:

> Life exists only in combustion, but the combustion which occurs in our own bodies, like that which takes place in our chimneys, leaves a detritus which is fatal to life. To remove this, we would administer lactic acid with ordinary

food. This acid is known to possess the power of removing or destroying the encrustations which form on the arteries, cartilages, and valves of the heart. As buttermilk abounds in this acid . . . [its habitual use] will free the system from these causes which inevitably cause death between the seventy-fifth and hundredth year.

Don't laugh. Look what happened to yogurt after word of the long-lived Russian peasants got out. Then there were all the people who took up the eating of cottage cheese because it too was believed to prolong life—mostly by preventing obesity, but incidentally to avoid fatty deposits in arteries. You do know, of course, that all cottage cheese is made from buttermilk.

For example, according to Elisabeth Luard in *The Old World Kitchen: The Rich Tradition of European Peasant Cooking* (Bantam Books, 1987), Holland's Hangop is a fresh buttermilk cheese with a thick, creamy, yogurtlike curd. Its name, meaning "hanged," comes from the practice of hanging up a pillowcase on a convenient branch for the buttermilk inside to drip out its whey.

Here is a formal recipe for cottage cheese, in case you wish to give it a try:

> Set a quantity of fresh milk in a moderately warm room and allow to sour naturally. Unless the milk has been contaminated at the barn or by a soiled utensil, the curd will be smooth, even, and free from gas bubbles. The best temperature to set milk for cottage cheese is 70 to 72 degrees Fahrenheit. As soon as the milk is curdled throughout, stir and break it up; then heat it gradually to 104 degrees. If you do not have a dairy thermometer, set the milk on the back of the stove so it will not be heated too much. When the whey separates from the curd, pour the curd into a muslin bag and hang up to drain.

My recipe-testing friend Bernard Oyer tells of a childhood memory of seeing a neighbor's wife hang sacks from her clothesline that dripped and dripped, and he could never figure out what she was doing. When we were discussing some of the uses of buttermilk, he made the connection: The woman was making her own cottage cheese.

> It takes from two to ten hours to drain the curd, depending on the size and firmnesss of the curd particles. When drained, it is moist and granular but not sticky. It should then be salted to taste; about one ounce of salt is sufficient for eight pounds of cheese.

Enough of uses, back to history. Circa 1850, as dairy products grew in popularity and profitability, commercialism brought on chicanery, especially the practice of watering down milk (which was bought by weight), an act labeled by newspapers of the day as "the marriage of cow to pump."

To give the watery concoction greater density, salt was added, plus burnt sugar helped to take away the "blue" tint that the water imparted.

The Shakers finally came up with a simple method of testing for this adulteration. They dipped a well-polished knitting needle into a deep vessel of the milk. When withdrawn, drops of pure milk would stick to the needle, while watered-down milk would run off it.

Other adulterants were tried over the years with fleeting success: powdered chalk and flour to thicken watered-down milk; various dyes to improve the color; coconut and other oils substituted for butterfat, which had been removed.

Buttermilk was no more immune to adulteration than butter. From the mid-1850s on, we come across motherly advice to daughters about buying buttermilk: "That which is sold in cities as buttermilk is often adulterated; therefore, be sure that you see yellow flecks of butter in the milk you have to buy." Naturally once it became known that consumers were looking for golden flecks, such flecks became commonplace among those out to make a quick buck from buttermilk. In your supermarket to this day, you will find cultured buttermilk made from skim milk that has had the tiniest soupçon of butterfat added to give that butter-flecked appearance.

Besides adulterating the product, chemists attempted to find cheap substitutes for butter. The first attempts in France were based on ground-up cows' udders—the idea may have been logical, but the result wasn't. Then, in the 1860s came a contribution of chemist Hippolyte Mege-Mouries, oleo-margarine—so named because it was supposedly made from the glycerides of oleic and margaric acids. It was called *butterine* in England, but this incensed the butter producers, and by act of Parliament in 1887, *margarine* became its official name.

In this country, dairymen fought the introduction of oleomargarine, but to no avail. By the end of the nineteenth century, Americans could easily buy margarine. The only problem with it was that it was the unpalatable color of lard. However, by act of Congress, margarine-makers were forbidden by law to dye their products. So they packed yellow-coloring packets with each package for women to use to color it themselves.

One hundred years after the first oleomargarine was introduced, a low-cholesterol margarine made with polyunsaturated fats was developed. Presently, and probably because of that, Americans buy more margarine than butter.

With the fat controversy gearing up again and hydrogenated oils taking a hit for being carcinogens, milk producers have found the time to be ripe to introduce another low-fat butter "substitute." Promoted as being made from sweet cream or sweet-cream buttermilk, no mention is made that these spreads are made—just like margarine— with hydrogenated oils! Yes, a dribble of cream, skim milk, and/or buttermilk is added, but in such small measure that, in the words of one manufacturer, it "adds a trivial amount of cholesterol." Commanding prices higher than plain margarine and close to those of real butter, these spreads entice us to enjoy the taste of butter but with 25 percent less fat. And they do so while delivering partially or completely hydrogenated oils.

But if you want real butter taste, 80 percent less saturated fat, and no hydrogenated oils, make your own genuinely buttery spread . . . with buttermilk.

How?

Through a butter better for you and better for cooking than regular butter or margarine or shortening or lard.

The French, inventors of margarine, would call this *faux beurre*, or fake butter. I call it Batter Butter™ and a lifesaver, for this is no fake. This is a butter *stretcher*. Made with real butter and dried buttermilk, it has the consistency of real unsalted butter. I personally can taste the difference, but I also know that others can't. (Nor can I in combination with other flavors.) Many of the recipes I have for spreads and dips originally called for sweet whipped butter, and when I cut back on the use of butter, I eliminated those dips from our table. No more. Now I replace the butter with Batter Butter. In cooking, I find that Batter Butter resolves the butter-margarine-shortening question without sacrificing flavor. Depending on the oil you use, it has only 42 to 47 percent of the calories in real butter and a mere 6.7 grams of fat per serving, of which 2.5 are saturated, as compared to butter's 11 grams, of which 7 are saturated. It cooks, tastes, enriches without fattening—does almost everything that real butter does while salving your conscience, too. The only difference I've found is that thanks to all the milk solids, it can't be used to sauté, but then we weight watchers shouldn't be frying foods anyway, should we?

Batter Butter

2 envelopes (½ ounce) unflavored gelatin

2 cups hot water

⅛ teaspoon salt

3 capsules (1,200 mg) lecithin (see Tips)

4 sticks (1 pound) unsalted butter, at room temperature

⅔ cup dried buttermilk powder (see Tips)

1⅓ cups corn, safflower, or other oil

Yellow food coloring (optional)

Additional salt (optional)

Dissolve the gelatin in the hot water with the salt. Allow to cool. (You can do this in the refrigerator if you keep checking on it, or at room temperature for 2 to 4 hours, depending on the heat of the room.) When the gelatin has cooled to the consistency of raw egg whites—thick yet still liquid—open the lecithin capsules and squeeze the contents into the gelatin mixture.

Cream the butter in the large bowl of your mixer at high speed until white and fluffy. Lower the speed and gradually add the dried buttermilk powder, then the oil. Very slowly blend in the gelatin-water-salt-lecithin mixture (you will have 3 cups). The result will be a very light color, that of shortening, so you might want to add food coloring. I use approximately 8 drops of yellow to get the color I want. (No, you're not cheating. Most real butter is artificially colored, too.)

If you are used to cooking with salted butter, add ¼ scant teaspoon salt to the Batter Butter, then taste before adding more.

Yield: 10 cups or 5 pounds of "stretched" butter. Store in one-cup or one-pound resealable containers and refrigerate. Let sit at room temperature for a few minutes before using. Freeze whatever you won't use in the next week because, like butter, this has no preservatives. Thaw before using.

Tips: Lecithin, a natural emulsifier and antioxidant, is available at health food stores. I have also found it in the vitamin section of my supermarket. Cutting the lecithin capsules open is the toughest part. Use a tea towel to hold one end of the capsule and just nick it, then squeeze out the contents, trying to get as much of the yellow goop as possible into the gelatin and off your hands. Don't try adding the whole capsules to the hot water—they won't totally disperse, nor will the contents. I know: I've tried it, and I've made a mess.

Dried buttermilk is available nationwide in supermarkets. Look for it in the section with dried milk or with cocoas. If you can't find it, call SACO, distributor of SACO Cultured Buttermilk Blend dried buttermilk, at 1-800-373-SACO.

When refrigerated, Batter Butter solidifies just like butter. It freezes, too, but should be allowed to thaw before using.

BAKING BUTTER

If you're not into do-it-yourself, another answer is Mrs. Bateman's Baking Butter. This is what I call low-low fat: only 13 grams of fat per cup instead of the 176 found in a cup of butter or 205 in a cup of shortening; 624 calories per cup compared to 1,633 in the same amount of butter and some margarines. Unfortunately, it is not available nationwide but can be ordered in five-pound tubs from Bateman's Baking Butter, Inc., 170 W. Main Street, Rigby, Idaho 83442 (208-745-9033). It requires some adapting for recipes other than in yeast breads. For example, it won't cream with sugar and doesn't melt like butter or margarine, but the finished results are excellent.

It may be that as you read this book, you begin to envision yourself buying buttermilk by the gallon. (You can't. It only comes by the quart.) So what would be more fitting than the most elementary substitution of them all: homemade for storebought buttermilk.

Homemade Buttermilk from Starter

Despite the fact that you'll find this recipe in hundreds upon hundreds of cookbooks, not to mention on the back of tens of thousands of boxes of dried nonfat milk, I doubt less than one cook in a thousand can make it successfully. (Please, don't take this as an aspersion on your ability. It is not. In fact, I count myself among the unsuccessful 999.)

Accept this as a fact of life: The dairy products we have in our supermarkets do not lend themselves to making homemade buttermilk, because although commercial buttermilks are cultured, they do not have the active cultures needed to multiply in low-fat or skim milk. Furthermore, because most milk is pasteurized, wild spores present in your kitchen won't have the time to multiply before the milk spoils. But if you can find the buttermilk with live cultures (see below) and use nonfat dried milk, you may be able to make your own starter.

1 quart fluid, reconstituted nonfat or low-fat dried milk
¹/₂ cup cultured buttermilk
Pinch of salt (optional)

The day before you wish to make the starter, reconstitute the dried milk. Because nonfat dried milk is 50 percent lactose, or milk sugar, which is not readily soluble, you need to give it at least 24 hours to rest in the refrigerator. Otherwise, it will be grainy and the cultures will not spread evenly throughout the mixture.

Bring reconstituted milk to room temperature and add room-temperature buttermilk. Let stand for 5 to 6 hours at room temperature. It should clabber, or thicken, and develop a somewhat strong sour but not spoiled odor. Stir once more. Add salt now if your storebought buttermilk starter is salt-free. Refrigerate.

Yield: 1 generous quart

Tip: If after those half-dozen hours, nothing has happened, it probably won't. Best to start over or give up—or advance to the next recipe.

HOMEMADE BUTTERMILK FROM LIVE CULTURES

If you think you'll be doing a lot of cooking with buttermilk, then it is wise to invest less than ten dollars in a vial of *fil mjölk*, a live Swedish buttermilk culture. (Available from Gem Cultures, 30301 Sherwood Road, Fort Bragg, CA 95437; 707-964-2922. Although they don't take credit cards, they will bill direct, and for the cost of the phone call, they'll send you a free catalog. Be sure to ask for Betty.)

Fil mjölk works like a sourdough starter: Make one batch, use most of it, and make another batch from what's left. Almost any dairy product can be cultured, but like all Swedes, the culture is temperature sensitive. It doesn't like temperatures over 80 degrees, so find a cool place in which to keep it. This is one product that keeps on giving: For that initial investment, you can have real buttermilk forever!

DRIED BUTTERMILK

If your only interest is in buttermilk for baking, most storebought buttermilks will do just fine. Or you can buy a powdered form of old-fashioned sweet-cream buttermilk in your supermarket. The bad news is that it doesn't have the tang of the real thing. The good news is that because it doesn't have the tang, it works better in some of your more delicately flavored recipes.

SACO Cultured Buttermilk Blend contains sweet-cream churned buttermilk, sweet dairy whey, sodium caseinate, and lactic acid—all natural products.

To use in place of fluid buttermilk in any baking recipe in this book, follow the recipe instructions as usual, except add the proper amount of dried buttermilk (see below) to the other dry ingredients. And when told to add liquid buttermilk, substitute the appropriate amount of water.

To substitute dried buttermilk for liquid:

3½ tablespoons (0.8 ounces) dry plus 1 cup water = 1 cup buttermilk

7 tablespoons (1.6 ounces) dry plus 2 cups water = 2 cups buttermilk

4 | *Starters*

BEVERAGES

Husband Arthur's Buttermilk

Lee's Border Buttermilk

Danish "Sweet Buttermilk"

Buttermilk Coolers

Fruit Coolers

Bloody Buttermilk

BUTTER SPREADS

Olive Butter

Roquefort Butter

Good-A-Butter

Shrimp Spread

Mustardy Shrimp Paste

APPETIZERS

Chicken Liver Terrine

Hot Chilled-Chicken-Liver Terrine

Bacon Buttermilk Dip

BEVERAGES

For years and years my husband's evening cocktail was a glass of buttermilk. By my calculations—allowing for parties and the like—that works out to more than three thousand quarts of buttermilk. Despite that, or maybe even because of it, his heart and arteries are in excellent shape.

So, if you too are looking for a cholesterol-free, alcohol-free drink, here is a sampling of buttermilk refreshers.

Husband Arthur's Buttermilk

He drinks it the old-fashioned way. By that I mean shaken not stirred, straight from the carton, and liberally salted and peppered. At first, I thought he was—well, strange—then I discovered he's not alone. This is how old-timers prefer it.

Lee's Border Buttermilk

Now this is my kind of buttermilk, and Texas is where they call it Border Buttermilk. It is the secret of our marriage. Arthur drinks his buttermilk, I drink this soothing tequila concoction that is smooth and frothy and milky-looking, and everyone's happy. P.S.: This is the only recipe in this book that does not contain buttermilk.

One 6-ounce can frozen lemonade concentrate
1 lemonade can tequila

Crush enough ice in a blender until it is at least half full. Add the lemonade and tequila, and some extra whole ice if necessary. Blend at high speed.

Yield: 4 glasses

Danish "Sweet Buttermilk"

Many people who think they wouldn't like to drink buttermilk enjoy this refreshingly tart milkshake, especially during the summer. I speak from experience. The first time I tried it, I was surprised at how good it was. In fact, I was almost converted, but not quite.

2 tablespoons sugar
1 large egg
2 cups buttermilk
1 tablespoon lemon juice

Blend all the ingredients in a blender until the egg is well incorporated and the sugar dissolved.

Yield: Two 1-cup servings

Tip: You should blend for a few minutes, long enough for the egg to partially cook through friction. In this day and age of salmonella warnings, you might want to make the milkshake in advance, then heat while stirring, and refrigerate before serving.

Buttermilk Coolers

I keep asking myself, if Arthur likes plain buttermilk so much, why does he keep searching out new buttermilk-based beverages? Variety, I suppose, is one answer. The thrill of discovery another. And coaxing me into drinking buttermilk under the guise of recipe-testing, that just might be another. (I prefer the orange or lemonade; he likes them all.)

One 6-ounce can frozen concentrated juice (orange,
    pineapple, lemonade, limeade, grape, or punch)
4 cups buttermilk

Let the concentrate juice thaw long enough to be mixable. Combine with the buttermilk. Use a blender to make it frothy.

FRUIT COOLERS
Mix equal parts buttermilk and nonconcentrated apple, orange, pineapple, or other juices.

BLOODY BUTTERMILK
Combine equal parts buttermilk and tomato or vegetable juice. Season with Tabasco, Worcestershire, salt, pepper, and lemon juice. Stir and serve with a celery stick.

BUTTER SPREADS

I confess to being an aficionado of Julie Dannenbaum, and I love her cookbooks. Unfortunately, she's a purist and calls for only the most expensive (and fat-enriched) ingredients. So until I discovered Batter Butter, I could only read but not taste. Now I can do both.

Olive Butter

This particular recipe is my downfall. I love it. But when made with real butter, it's simply too rich for me. That's why I converted the recipe to Batter Butter. It goes together like a dream, especially if you have a food processor.

One 16-ounce can pitted black olives, drained
2 garlic cloves, finely chopped
One 1-inch piece anchovy paste or 6 anchovy fillets,
    drained
1 cup Batter Butter, at room temperature (page 25)
½ teaspoon pepper
Salt (optional)
1 package anisette toast
1 package white radishes, cleaned, derooted, detopped

Chop the black olives finely. Mince the garlic cloves and anchovy fillets, if using.

Cream the Batter Butter. Add the olives, garlic, anchovy paste or fillets, and pepper. Taste to see if it needs salt. (If using plain Batter Butter, it probably will. Start with a meager pinch.) Pack the mixture into a serving mold or crock.

Serve chilled or at room temperature, with anisette toast and/or white radishes.

Yield: 2 cups

Tip: You can add 1 teaspoon anisette or any other licorice-flavored liqueur to the Batter Butter and serve with plain crackers or melba toast.

Roquefort Butter

This is for all true Roquefort lovers: If you cannot find Roquefort in the store, substitute blue cheese, which many prefer to Roquefort anyway and is much less expensive. Once all the ingredients are at room temperature, the spread goes together quickly, especially in a mini–food processor, and may be prepared in advance.

½ **cup Batter Butter, at room temperature (page 25)**

6 to 8 ounces Roquefort cheese

1 tablespoon cognac

Pinch of cayenne pepper

1 teaspoon finely chopped parsley (optional)

Brush a 1-cup mold with vegetable oil.

Beat the Batter Butter in a mixer, then add the Roquefort, bit by bit. Continue beating until the mixture is fluffy, 3 to 5 minutes. Add the cognac, cayenne, and parsley, if desired. Pack into the mold. Chill for several hours or overnight.

Yield: 6 servings, unmolded and served with crackers

Tip: I use a plastic 1-cup margarine tub as a mold; it is not really necessary to oil it.

Good-A-Butter

Forgive the pun. If you can't get Gouda, use Edam. Make this at least one day in advance so the flavors blend. It will make up nice and fluffy and delicious but will not be butter-smooth because of the cheese.

7 ounces Gouda or Edam cheese
⅓ cup Batter Butter (page 25)
¾ tablespoon cognac
⅛ to ¼ teaspoon cayenne pepper
Salt and pepper

Bring the cheese and Batter Butter to room temperature. Chop the cheese into small pieces.

Beat the chopped cheese in the mixer bowl until it is creamy, along with the cognac and cayenne. This may take as long as 10 minutes unless you are using a heavy-duty mixer with a flat whip. Add the Batter Butter, a dollop at a time, until all is incorporated. This will go fast. Adjust the seasonings, adding more cayenne if you like things spicy. Mound the mixture in a bowl, sprinkle cayenne (or cheat and use paprika) on top, and serve chilled.

Yield: 6 servings

Tip: Although I love this spread, I haven't the patience to do it in a mixer. I use a mini–food processor and dump everything into it.

For a more impressive presentation, increase the recipe based on the size of the cheese ball you buy. Then hollow out the cheese ball and use it as a serving piece.

Shrimp Spread

There are times when serving a bowl of fresh shrimp just isn't convenient, financially. A less expensive, equally nonfattening version is this shrimp spread. But it tastes, looks, and sounds impressive.

2 pounds small shrimp
½ cup Batter Butter (page 25)
Up to 3 tablespoons low-fat mayonnaise
¼ teaspoon lemon juice
Pinch of mace
1 teaspoon Worcestershire sauce
1 or 2 drops red pepper sauce, or more to taste
Salt and pepper

If the shrimp is not precooked, boil in salted water and peel.

Process the shrimp in a food processor and add the Batter Butter and enough mayonnaise to bind together and soften. Season well with lemon juice, ground mace, Worcestershire and red pepper sauces, salt and pepper.

Serve chilled.

Yield: 1 cup

Tip: If you don't have mace, you can eliminate it or replace it with celery seed.

MUSTARDY SHRIMP PASTE

Eliminate mayonnaise and replace with ¼ teaspoon dry mustard, 10 drops onion juice, and 1 tablespoon dry sherry.

APPETIZERS

Chicken Liver Terrine

This version of the ever-popular party dish is something between a pâté and a mousse—and between a mousse and a butter. In any event, it's delicious. Delicious enough for guests to ask for the recipe. Which gets complicated because the secret of this dish is Batter Butter!

1 pound chicken livers
1 cup unsalted chicken stock
½ cup roughly chopped onion
½ teaspoon salt
¼ teaspoon pepper
2 cups Batter Butter (page 25)
1 tablespoon or more cognac

Trim the chicken livers of all fat and place them in a large saucepan with the stock, onion, salt, and pepper. Bring to a boil, reduce the heat, and simmer for 12 to 15 minutes, or until the livers are cooked through. Strain and let cool. Bring the unsalted Batter Butter to room temperature.

Process the chicken livers with the Batter Butter in a food processor. When it starts coming together, add the cognac. Transfer to a refrigerator bowl. Chill covered, stirring occasionally, until the mixture begins to thicken. Then transfer to a serving dish.

Serve chilled. This can be frozen, but thaw before serving.

Yield: 2 cups

Tip: Remember, chilling will deaden the flavor, so be sure to add enough cognac.

HOT CHILLED-CHICKEN-LIVER TERRINE

Now that everybody's into salsa and buffalo wings, the regular version of this may be too tame for you. So try adding hot pepper sauce to the mixture before chilling—this can be anywhere from ½ to 1 teaspoon or more, depending on how spicy you like it. If it gets too spicy, add more cognac.

Bacon Buttermilk Dip

True connoisseurs of buffalo wings know that the best way to intensify the hot spiciness of wings is by combining it with a cooling dip, in this case one made with buttermilk, bacon, and cucumber, or you can substitute the more traditional blue cheese.

1 garlic clove, crushed

1 large cucumber

2 slices bacon

1 tablespoon finely chopped onion

1 tablespoon flour

½ cup buttermilk, or more as needed

Salt and pepper

Peel and crush the garlic. Peel, slice, and dice the cucumber and soak it in cold, salted water to draw out the bitterness. Before mixing the cucumber into the dip, remove and squeeze out any excess water.

Fry the bacon in a small skillet over moderate heat until barely crisp. Remove the bacon—reserve the grease—drain, crumble, and put aside. Add the onion and garlic to the bacon fat and cook until softened, less than 1 minute. Add the flour to the pan and combine well, then slowly add the buttermilk. Continue cooking over low heat until thickened. Remove from the heat and add the crumbled bacon and salt and pepper. Stir in the drained and squeezed cucumber. Keep warm.

Serve with buffalo wings or celery sticks.

Yield: ½ cup or enough for 4 servings of wings

Tip: If you're a microwaver of bacon, go right ahead, but don't sandwich the bacon between sheets of paper towels. Instead, do bacon in a glass pie plate and cover with waxed paper or a lid in order to reserve the fat.

BLUE CHEESE DIP
Substitute 3 ounces blue cheese, crumbled, for the cucumber.

5 | Soups

Cucumber-Vichyssoise Soup

Fruit Soup

Carrot Soup

Winter Carrot Soup

Summer Carrot Soup

Creamless Cream of Tomato Soup

Cream of Gazpacho

Pink Beet Soup

Chinese Curdled Pink Beet Soup

Strawberry Burgundy Soup

Shrimp Bisque

Real Cream of Shrimp Soup

Lobster Bisque

Cream of Cheese Soup

No Cook Tomato-Avocado Soup

Chilled Uncooked Vegetable Soup

Generally speaking, most buttermilk soups are served chilled, but they need not be. The problem is that unless cooked at very low temperatures, buttermilk may curdle. If that should happen, the taste won't be affected.

Buttermilk in soup offers the same emulsifiers that cream has but without all the fat. That's why you can use buttermilk in place of sour cream provided you also incorporate 2 tablespoons flour or 1 tablespoon cornstarch.

Mollie Katzen, author of the vegetarian *Moosewood Cookbook*, suggests whisking in some buttermilk to a soup at the very last minute, just as the French add a dollop of butter and for the same reason: to bind, to blend, to enhance.

Cucumber-Vichyssoise Soup

Served cold, this pale green soup makes a marvelous vichyssoise, its flavors blending together so that none totally dominates. Served warm, it's a potato soup with a subtly different taste, which will have guests guessing even while clamoring for more. Garnish with croutons or chopped chives.

1 large baking potato

1 large cucumber

2 cups chicken stock, plus water as needed to cover

2 large scallions

1/2 tablespoon butter or margarine

1 cup buttermilk

1 tablespoon cornstarch

1/2 teaspoon salt or to taste

1/4 teaspoon pepper (white is nice if you have it)

Peel the potato and slice 1/2-inch thick lengthwise, then cut crosswise into 1/2-inch slices. Peel and slice the cucumber the same way.

Cook the potato and cucumber slices in a 1 1/2-quart saucepan with the chicken stock (add additional water if necessary to cover). Sauté the scallions in the butter or margarine in a small frying pan until soft and lightly browned and add to the saucepan. Simmer for 20 minutes or until the potatoes are tender. Puree the potato-cucumber-scallion mixture in a blender or food processor and return to the pan.

Combine the buttermilk and cornstarch and add to the soup. Heat gently for a few minutes (do not boil) and correct the seasonings if serving hot. If planning to serve as vichyssoise, chill for several hours, then correct the seasonings; you will probably need to add some salt.

Yield: Four 6-ounce servings

Tip: Always add buttermilk to the cornstarch (or flour or arrowroot), not vice versa. To be more authentically French, substitute shallots for scallions.

Fruit Soup

Being Scandinavian, my concept of fruit soups was old-fashioned. I thought such soups had to be made with dried fruit, cooked, strained, and a lot more work than they're worth. But a visit to a restaurant in Skippack, Pennsylvania, first introduced me to this modern, no-less low-cal, much easier, just as delicious chilled version.

1 fresh peach or 2 apricots, peeled and chopped

1 medium banana

¹/₂ cup applesauce

3 cups unsweetened fruit juice—orange, grape, apple, etc.

1 cup buttermilk

Juice from 1 lemon (2 tablespoons)

2 or 3 tablespoons honey or brown sugar (or more, if needed)

¹/₂ teaspoon cinnamon, nutmeg, allspice, and/or dried mint (optional)

Peel and dice the peach or apricots. Puree with banana and applesauce in a blender with the fruit juice, buttermilk, and lemon juice.

Sweeten to taste with honey or brown sugar. Add seasonings if you wish.

Chill before serving.

Yield: 4 large or 6 small servings

Tip: You can make this soup thicker or thinner by increasing or decreasing the size of the banana you use—the bigger, the thicker. Also, if you don't have any applesauce, use 1 medium apple, peeled, cored, and finely chopped.

You can use strawberries or any other assertively flavored fruit. *Exception:* I've tried it with blueberries; it tastes good but looks terrible.

Carrot Soup

This soup can be either hearty-bland or refreshingly light and sweet, depending on the freshness of the carrots.

2 pounds carrots

4 cups water

1 to 2 teaspoons sugar

1 teaspoon salt

1 cup chopped onion

1 or 2 small garlic cloves, crushed

3 tablespoons butter or margarine

1 cup buttermilk

1 teaspoon grated horseradish

1 teaspoon grated ginger root

Scrub and coarsely chop the carrots. Place the carrots in a medium-sized pot and cover with water. Add the sugar—more for older carrots, less for younger ones—and salt. Bring to a boil, then simmer until the carrots are fork-tender, about 15 minutes. Let cool to room temperature.

Sauté the onion and garlic in the butter until the onion is soft and turns transparent. Combine the carrots, onion, and garlic and puree in a blender. When this has been thoroughly pureed, return to the pot and whisk in the buttermilk over low heat. Heat very slowly. At the last minute add the horseradish and ginger root.

Yield: 4 servings

Tip: Hot liquids expand more when pureed in a blender. So, if you choose not to cool the ingredients, puree only 1 cup at a time, using a Pyrex measuring cup for scooping out the carrot mixture.

WINTER CARROT SOUP
Eliminate the sugar and replace with 1 medium potato, peeled and chopped. Add $1/2$ teaspoon each marjoram and basil.

SUMMER CARROT SOUP
Add ½ cup coarsely chopped almonds to the onion-garlic mixture and sauté. Replace the horseradish and ginger root with ¼ teaspoon cinnamon and ⅛ teaspoon nutmeg.

Creamless Cream of Tomato Soup

Not so thick as regular canned soup made with milk, but it's much better and almost as simple.

1 small carrot
1 tablespoon chopped chives
6 ripe tomatoes, peeled, or 1 large can (28 ounces) plum
    tomatoes
1 shallot, minced
2 garlic cloves
½ cup water
2 cups buttermilk
Salt

Peel and julienne the carrot and chop the chives for the garnish.

Cook the tomatoes, shallot, and garlic in water for 15 minutes, and put through a food processor or blender (strain for finer texture). Add the buttermilk, season with salt to taste, and chill. Garnish with the carrot and chives.

To serve it authentically, put one or two ice cubes in each soup bowl before serving. Sprinkle with parsley and/or buttered bread crumbs.

Yield: 6 servings

Tip: To peel tomatoes, pierce each at the stem end and hold for 20 seconds in boiling water. The skin should simply slip off.

CREAM OF GAZPACHO
Add ½ cup chopped green pepper, 1 small cucumber, peeled and chopped, and ½ cup chopped watercress to the mixture before putting through the blender.

Pink Beet Soup

Today, we understand borscht to be a meat-based beet soup that may contain other vegetables, such as cabbage. However, in Russia, it was originally made from the "cow parsnip," a member of the carrot family. Lacking cow parsnips, this version is less authentic but, to my way of thinking, better tasting. In fact, it is so pretty, so refreshing, so festive, so light, you may give up old-fashioned borscht forever.

6 small fresh beets

1 large cucumber

3 scallions

1½ cups water

1 tablespoon sugar

1 tablespoon raspberry vinegar (or cider vinegar)

1½ cups buttermilk

Salt and freshly ground white pepper

1 tablespoon minced fresh dill

Remove the tops and roots of the beets. Peel and grate the beets and place in a large non-aluminum saucepan. Peel the cucumber, cut it in half, scoop out the seeds and discard them, and chop finely or coarsely grate. Remove the dark green tops from the onions and reserve. Mince the white and light green parts of the onions, and add the onions and the cucumber to the beets.

Cover with water and add the sugar. Bring to a boil, reduce the heat, and simmer until the cucumber and beets are tender, 15 to 20 minutes. Remove from the heat and cool to room temperature. Whisk in the vinegar and buttermilk. Season with salt and pepper. Cover and chill for approximately 3 hours.

Serve in soup plates. Garnish with a sprinkling of minced dark green onions and dill.

Yield: 6 medium-size servings

Tip: Instead of fresh beets, use 24 ounces canned beets (not Harvard), well drained. Add to the cucumber mixture about 15 minutes into cooking.

CHINESE CURDLED PINK BEET SOUP
Cold buttermilk has a tendency to curdle if you add it while soup is hot, which won't affect the taste but will alter the appearance. If this should happen, rename the soup and serve anyway, but with lots of garnish floating on top.

Strawberry Burgundy Soup

This soup is so good that it almost deserves to be placed in the dessert chapter.

3 pints strawberries
1 cup water
½ cup sugar
½ cup all-purpose flour
2 cups burgundy wine
2 cups orange juice
4 cups buttermilk

Reserve 6 strawberries for garnish. Wash and hull the remainder, and depending on their size, roughly half or quarter them. Cook the strawberries in water for 10 minutes.

In a separate saucepan, combine the sugar, flour, wine, and orange juice. Bring to a boil over medium heat, whisking gently, about 10 minutes. Combine the strawberries and the thickened mixture. Puree in a blender and cool to room temperature. Stir in the buttermilk. Chill.

Serve garnished with strawberry slices and mint leaves, if desired. A nice garnish is a whole strawberry, hull and all, sliced partially through, fanned out, and placed in the center of the soup.

Yield: 6 servings

Tip: When combining wet and dry ingredients, add the wet to the dry.

Shrimp Bisque

This buttermilk-based cream of shrimp soup is even better than the canned version and equally versatile.

2½ **pounds cooked shrimp**
4 **tablespoons butter**
4 **tablespoons flour**
4 **cups buttermilk**
Salt and pepper
Sherry (optional)

Clean the shrimp and chop coarsely or, if you wish to be extra fancy, grind into a paste in a food processor.

Melt the butter in the top of a double boiler over direct heat and then add the flour to make a roux. Add the buttermilk. Place over hot water and cook slowly until thickened. Add the shrimp and cook slowly until the shrimp are warmed through. Add the salt and pepper to taste. Just before serving, add a splash of sherry to each bowl, if desired.

Yield: 8 servings

Tip: Buy supermarket shrimp on sale (often 70 or more to a pound) for this soup. If they're frozen, they frequently come already cooked and shelled, in which case I neither chop nor grind but add as is.

REAL CREAM OF SHRIMP SOUP
Add 2 cups whole cream when you add the buttermilk.

LOBSTER BISQUE
If you ever wondered what to do with the carcass of a whole lobster once you've used the tail, here's the perfect answer. Remove any large pieces of meat from the lobster carcass. Cook the rest, including the coral and roe, in buttermilk in a double boiler over boiling hot water for about 30 minutes. Strain into a bowl. In a separate saucepan, make the roux of the butter and flour. Add the strained buttermilk plus the pieces of lobster meat and cream if you wish. Cook over low heat just until the lobster is warmed through.

Cream of Cheese Soup

An interesting twist on French onion soup. This time the cheese is on the bottom. It is a hearty meal in itself and, unlike real French onion soup, is not as calorie-rich as it appears, thanks to the buttermilk.

1 cup (4 ounces) sharp cheddar cheese

1 Bermuda onion, sliced thin

One 2-inch piece of carrot

1 medium onion

4 cups buttermilk, at room temperature

4 tablespoons butter

4 tablespoons flour

2 egg yolks

1/4 teaspoon mace

Salt and pepper

6 rounds white bread, toasted

Mozzarella cheese (optional)

Dice or grate the cheddar cheese (reserve a few of tablespoons for final presentation if you don't plan to use the mozzarella). Fry the onion until soft and golden brown, and reserve.

Cook the carrot and onion in the buttermilk over low heat until the vegetables are tender, stirring frequently so as not to burn the milk. Remove the vegetables. In the top of a double boiler, melt the butter and add the flour to make a roux. Add the buttermilk. Place over medium heat and stir until thickened—which should happen almost immediately. Remove from the heat and pour a small quantity into the beaten egg yolks to bring them up to temperature. Return the thickened egg yolk–buttermilk mixture to the double boiler and add the seasonings, stirring with a whisk until the mixture thickens some more. Add the cheese and stir until the cheese melts. Season to taste.

Serve hot, topped with toasted rounds piled high with sautéed onions and sprinkled with cheese—either reserved cheddar or mozzarella. This can be reheated in a double boiler or microwaved on low.

Yield: 6 servings

Tip: If you don't object to having pieces of carrot and onion in the soup, this soup can go together almost impossibly fast: Puree the raw onion and carrot in a food processor with some of the buttermilk before heating them with the rest of the buttermilk. Strain the buttermilk as you stir it into the roux if you wish.

No Cook Tomato-Avocado Soup

This is a particularly happy combination of flavors. The acidic qualities of the tomatoes and buttermilk are balanced by the bland, fatty taste and texture of the avocado. This goes together fast if you use a food processor.

3 pounds (8 medium) tomatoes

1 ripe avocado, peeled and seeded

Juice of ½ lemon

2 tablespoons tomato paste

1 cup buttermilk

Salt and pepper

Tabasco or hot pepper sauce

2 tablespoons finely minced fresh parsley

1 small cucumber, peeled, seeded, and diced

Sour cream, plain yogurt, or crème fraîche (optional)

Peel the tomatoes by piercing with a fork and dipping in boiling water for 20 seconds. Cut each tomato in half and squeeze out the seeds—no need to be thorough.

Puree the tomatoes in a food processor or blender and press the pulp through a strainer to remove any seeds. Puree the avocado in the food processor with the lemon juice and recombine with the pureed tomatoes, tomato paste, and buttermilk. Pulse until smooth. Season to taste with salt and pepper and a few drops of Tabasco. Refrigerate for several hours, covered, before serving. Retaste and recorrect seasonings.

For an impressive company dish, serve in individual chilled bowls, garnish with diced cucumber, sprinkled with parsley or dollops of sour cream, yogurt, or crème fraîche.

Yield: 8 servings

Tip: If you're really pressed for time, don't bother to peel or seed the tomatoes—simply puree and strain. And if you're really, really pressed for time, don't bother to strain.

CHILLED UNCOOKED VEGETABLE SOUP
Add the bulbs and white parts of 4 small scallions, 1 seeded green pepper, and 1 small carrot to the food processor when pureeing the avocado.

6 | Salads and Salad Dressings

Cheesy Buttermilk Slaw

Coleslaw with Almonds

Plain Buttermilk Slaw

Raisin-Apple Slaw

Overnight Potato Salad

Cucumber Condiment/Salad Dressing

"Ranch" Cucumber Salad Dressing

Buttermilk Herb Dressing

Buttermilk Mayonnaise

Creamy Green Herb Dressing

Chile-Hot Salad Dressing

Creamy Italian Buttermilk Dressing

Creamy French Dressing

Savory French Dressing

Blue Cheese Dressing

Horseradish Sauce and/or Dressing

Apple Dressing

Fruit Dressing

Pineapple Cottage Cheese Dressing

Avocado Dressing

Buttermilk is a chameleon when it comes to flavor. On its own, it has an assertive taste. In combination, it yields to other flavors. For example, one of the classic flavor combinations of all time is cucumber and sour cream, usually to the detriment of the cucumber, which is overwhelmed by the sour cream. Not so buttermilk, which enhances the cuke's flavor and even reinforces its naturally delicate color. In other words, buttermilk makes other flavors even better.

Years ago, Calvin Trillin wrote about smuggling packets of buttermilk ranch dressing from the Midwest to the East as a favor for a friend. You should know that ranch dressing is simply a creamy dressing made with buttermilk. Try substituting buttermilk for one-third of the oil in your favorite dressing recipe. You'll see that the result will be a creamy version with fewer calories than you'd expect.

As you may have guessed by now, I'm not a purist. But I won't eat something that contains an ingredient I can't pronounce. So, if you're like me, you might want to try "buttermilk mayonnaise." It has several advantages over the real thing: First, it always sets up because it's cooked; second, no chance of salmonella poisoning; third, it's a good compromise between Miracle Whip and mayonnaise, which can reduce hassles in some houses.

Cheesy Buttermilk Slaw

You can use your favorite coleslaw recipe, or even the coleslaw mixture in the produce department, or try this cheesy one.

4 cups finely shredded cabbage (approximate)
1/2 cup grated American cheese
1 teaspoon dry mustard
1 tablespoon brown sugar
1/2 to 1 teaspoon salt
1/2 teaspoon paprika (optional)
Dash of red pepper
1 cup buttermilk
1 to 2 tablespoons cider vinegar
Green pepper, carrot, and pimiento, for garnish (optional)

If doing your own shredding, remove the hard core from the cabbage before you shred it. Mix the cabbage and American cheese in a large serving bowl. Combine the remaining ingredients in a separate bowl in the order given, using first the smaller portion of an ingredient, then tasting, and then, if necessary, using the larger amount.

Pour the dressing over the cabbage and mix well. Garnish with green pepper rings, julienne carrot strips, and pieces of pimiento.

Yield: 6 generous servings

Tip: Shred the cabbage in a food processor with a slicing blade. Or, if you like your coleslaw of the chopped variety, process in a blender with water to cover, then drain off the water.

COLESLAW WITH ALMONDS

Add about 1 cup slivered almonds to the dressing. To make the slaw more colorful, add julienne carrots, celery, and/or green peppers. For a truly interesting flavor combination, add crushed pineapple.

Plain Buttermilk Slaw

A colorful slaw that can be made ahead of time and mixed together about an hour before serving.

SLAW

1 small head (about 1 pound) cabbage, quartered and cored

1 small red onion

1 small carrot

DRESSING

¼ cup buttermilk

¼ cup sour cream

1 tablespoon cider vinegar

1 teaspoon Worcestershire

2 to 4 dashes hot sauce

1¼ teaspoons sugar

1 teaspoon celery seed

½ teaspoon salt

½ teaspoon freshly ground pepper

¼ cup chopped parsley

2 tablespoons chopped fresh basil (optional)

Thinly slice or mince (remember the old pepper-slaw made by Horn & Hardart?) the quartered and cored cabbage. Do likewise to the onion and carrot so that all components are of one size. Refrigerate until just before serving.

Combine all the ingredients for the dressing and whisk together and refrigerate for 2 to 24 hours.

Combine the slaw and dressing in a large bowl. Sprinkle with the parsley and chopped fresh basil, if desired.

Yield: 6 servings

Tips: Mince the cabbage, onion, and carrot in a food processor or, in combination with water, in a blender. If the latter, drain well before using.

For the dressing, I use an empty peanut-butter jar that has liquid measurements on the side to do both the measuring/mixing and the storing/chilling.

RAISIN-APPLE SLAW

I have been known to toss a handful of raisins and/or minced apple into the mixture just before serving. The acid in the vinegar and buttermilk keeps the apple from changing color.

Overnight Potato Salad

This is one of those do-in-advance recipes that get better with standing—and that can take some of the pressure out of picnic and barbecue preparing.

1 cup Buttermilk Mayonnaise, still hot (page 63)

4 cups diced boiled potatoes

3 tablespoons minced onion

2 tablespoons minced green pepper

3 tablespoons chopped cucumber or dill pickle

½ cup chopped celery hearts

3 sliced hard-boiled eggs

1 minced pimiento

The day before serving, make the Buttermilk Mayonnaise and keep warm over boiling water. Have all the vegetables ready. Boil the potatoes with the skins on until tender. Drain and, as soon as possible, remove the skins and dice the potatoes.

Combine with the other ingredients and pour the hot dressing over it—but don't drown the potatoes. Let the salad stand overnight in the refrigerator to blend the flavors. The next day, if the potatoes have absorbed most of the dressing, add more; it doesn't need to be hot.

Yield: 6 servings

Tip: It's easy to skin potatoes when they're hot if you spear each with a fork first and then peel.

Cucumber Condiment/Salad Dressing

Use as a side dish or a salad dressing. It goes especially well with ham, and it can be made well ahead of time.

4 cups peeled, seeded, and thinly sliced cucumbers
    (3 medium or 2 large)
1 tablespoon salt (approximate)
2 large scallions, minced (bulb and top, not leaves)
½ cup buttermilk
1 teaspoon minced dill (optional)

Slice the cucumbers as thin as possible. (Use your food processor or one of those slice-all gadgets advertised on TV or, if your kitchen is really well equipped, a French mandolin.) Put the slices on a large dinner plate (concave, not flat) and sprinkle with 2 teaspoons of the salt. (This will force the cucumbers to disgorge their juice, which can be bitter.) Place another dinner plate on top of the cucumbers. Place a weight on top. Let sit at room temperature for an hour. Then pour off the excess liquid and stir the cucumbers. Sprinkle the top layer with ½ teaspoon of the remaining salt. Repeat in 30 minutes. At the end of 2 hours, drain in a strainer or colander and rinse off the salt. Squeeze to remove excess water (I use both hands).

Combine with the other ingredients. Chill for several hours.

Yield: A little more than 1 cup

Tip: After rinsing, taste to be sure all dissolved salt is gone.

"RANCH" CUCUMBER SALAD DRESSING
Whir the above dressing in a blender for 20 to 30 seconds. Keeps in the refrigerator up to 2 weeks. Shake well before using.

Buttermilk Herb Dressing

There's nothing simpler to make. A noncooked dressing that's creamy but practically fat-free! Add your favorite herbs to vary it.

½ cup cider vinegar

1 tablespoon salad oil

1 teaspoon salt

⅛ teaspoon white pepper

1 cup buttermilk

1 teaspoon fresh or ½ teaspoon dried herbs, such as dillweed

½ teaspoon dry mustard, curry, or chopped garlic (optional)

Combine all the ingredients in a jar with a tight-fitting lid. Shake to blend the ingredients well and use as a dressing on a mix of crisp green salad leaves or cabbage.

Yield: 1½ cups

Tip: Never use "white" vinegar for anything but cleaning. Unlike cider vinegar, white is simply a mixture of chemicals.

Buttermilk Mayonnaise

Nothing cured me faster of buying "fat-free mayonnaise" than reading the ingredients label. Sure, you get one-tenth the number of calories, but real mayonnaise doesn't contain xanthan gum, sodium benzoate, potassium sorbate, and calcium disodium EDTA—the same preservative used in blood vials.

This cooked dressing is all natural! And naturally low in calories, naturally low in cholesterol, especially if you use the egg whites. The scant tablespoon of butter—about 100 calories—adds fewer than 5 calories per serving or a tablespoon of dressing, or substitute Batter Butter.

2 tablespoons flour or 1 tablespoon cornstarch

½ teaspoon salt

1 scant teaspoon dry mustard

1 tablespoon sugar

Cayenne pepper

¾ cup buttermilk

1 egg, well beaten, or ¼ cup egg whites

1 scant tablespoon butter or Batter Butter (page 25)

2 tablespoons cider vinegar

Fill the bottom of a double boiler with water almost to the level of the insert; heat until boiling.

Mix the dry ingredients and blend in a small amount of the buttermilk until the mixture is smooth. Put in the top of the double boiler with the rest of the buttermilk and the beaten egg. Cook over boiling water until mixture has thickened, stirring constantly. Add the butter and vinegar, blend well, and cool.

This may be easily doubled or tripled. Use in Waldorf, potato, coleslaw, and macaroni salads.

Yield: 1 cup

Tip: You can use this in place of nonfat mayonnaise in any recipe. And, of course, the reverse is true: You can use nonfat mayonnaise in any of my recipes.

Creamy Green Herb Dressing

If you've been looking for a ranch dressing just like the kind in the stores, this one comes the closest.

1/2 **cup reduced-calorie mayonnaise**
2/3 **cup water (approximate)**
3 **tablespoons dried buttermilk**
2 **garlic cloves, crushed**
1 **tablespoon chopped fresh parsley**
1 **tablespoon chopped fresh chives**

Put all the ingredients in a blender and whir, adding water as needed.

Or, to 1/2 cup reduced-calorie mayonnaise, add the buttermilk, garlic, parsley, and chives. Thin with more water to desired consistency.

Yield: 1 cup

Chile-Hot Salad Dressing

A dressing with bite. It goes great with Tex-Mex foods.

1/4 **cup diced green chiles**
3 **tablespoons Buttermilk Mayonnaise (page 63)**
Juice of 1/2 **lime**
1 **teaspoon sugar**
1/2 **teaspoon salt**
1 **clove garlic, crushed**
1 **cup buttermilk, well shaken**

Combine everything but the buttermilk in a blender or food processor. When the mixture is smooth, stir in the buttermilk. Chill until ready to serve.

Yield: A little over 1 cup

Tip: Although lime juice is best, you can substitute lemon juice, but not ounce for ounce. Although lime juice is far more acidic than lemon, a lime also contains less juice. So use a scant tablespoon of lemon juice.

Creamy Italian Buttermilk Dressing

Here is another way to use Buttermilk Mayonnaise (page 63), but you can, if you desire, use a low-fat commercial mayonnaise. I don't think there's a salad dressing more basic and more generally liked than this.

9 tablespoons (½ cup plus 1 tablespoon) buttermilk
5 tablespoons (¼ cup plus 1 tablespoon) low-fat mayonnaise
1 tablespoon grated onion
¼ teaspoon pepper
¼ to ½ teaspoon salt
1 garlic clove, minced, or ¼ teaspoon garlic powder
¼ teaspoon dried whole thyme or parsley
Dash of curry (optional)

Mix all the ingredients together in the order mentioned.

Yield: ¾ cup

Tip: Rather than actually grating the onion, scrape across it with a sharp knife until you have 1 tablespoon of pulp.

Creamy French Dressing

A variation on a traditional vinaigrette. It will be creamy, but not the orange-red color Americans seem to expect of "French dressing." I suggest you taste it before adding the sugar. You may decide it's fine as is.

2 tablespoons buttermilk

⅓ cup oil

2 tablespoons cider vinegar or lemon juice

½ teaspoon salt

¼ teaspoon paprika

⅛ teaspoon pepper

½ teaspoon sugar (optional)

Put all the ingredients except the sugar in a jar or stoppered bottle. Shake well and taste to determine whether or not to add sugar. Just before serving, shake vigorously to get the oil and vinegar to blend to form a thick emulsion.

This recipe can be doubled or tripled. It keeps well in the refrigerator.

Yield: ½ cup

Savory French Dressing

In other words, orange-colored French dressing. Add 1 tablespoon ketchup to the mixture. Depending on how acidic the ketchup is, the sugar may be an absolute necessity.

Blue Cheese Dressing

Simple, simple, simple! Yet it tastes as good or better than the blue cheese dressing served in restaurants at an expensive premium.

3 ounces blue cheese
1/2 cup buttermilk, or more as needed
1/2 teaspoon salt
1/4 teaspoon red pepper
4 drops Tabasco

Let the blue cheese come to room temperature. Mix the blue cheese with the buttermilk, and add the salt, pepper, and Tabasco. Let stand a few minutes. Add additional buttermilk if necessary so that it has a pouring thickness.

Yield: 1 cup

Tip: You'll get more blue cheese taste if you don't refrigerate the dressing before serving.

Horseradish Sauce and/or Dressing

Excellent with seafood, beef, and even with oyster crackers.

1 cup buttermilk
1 tablespoon cream-style prepared white horseradish, or
    more as needed
2 tablespoons lemon juice
1 teaspoon dry mustard
2 tablespoons chopped fresh parsley
1 teaspoon capers, without juice (optional)

Combine all the ingredients in order. Stir well and taste. Add more horseradish if necessary. Cover and refrigerate until needed. Taste again. (Chilling deadens the flavors.)

Yield: 1 1/4 cups

Tip: Unlike many condiments, horseradish does not grow stronger in taste as it ages, but weaker. The flavor of this sauce will mellow as it sits.

Apple Dressing

This is an excellent dressing for fruit salad; it's best described as sweet-sour.

4 tablespoons arrowroot

¼ cup sugar

1 cup apple juice

Juice of 1 lemon

1 cup buttermilk

1 egg, well beaten

¼ teaspoon salt

Bring water to a boil in a double boiler.

Place the arrowroot and sugar in the top of the double boiler and mix well. Add the apple juice, lemon juice, and buttermilk and mix until smooth. Cook until thick, stirring frequently. Add the beaten egg and cook for 5 minutes over low heat, stirring constantly. Add the salt and cook only long enough for the salt to dissolve, less than a minute.

Yield: 1½ cups

Tip: When combining eggs and hot liquids, gradually add the hot liquid to the egg to partially cook the egg. Then return the mixture to the pan to cook until thick.

FRUIT DRESSING

Substitute any fruit juice—cranberry, apricot, etc.—that makes a happy combination with buttermilk; however, I wouldn't try grapefruit juice.

Pineapple Cottage Cheese Dressing

Serve this thinned down to pouring thickness to use on any kind of mixed fruit salad. Or keep it thick and use it as a dip with potato chips. In either case, the buttermilk helps blend the flavors together while counteracting some of the sweetness of the pineapple.

1 pound pineapple cottage cheese
Buttermilk

Prepare 4 to 24 hours in advance of serving.

   Place the cottage cheese in a blender and add ¼ cup buttermilk to start. Keep adding buttermilk until you achieve the consistency you want. Chill before serving.

Yield: About 2 cups

Tip: When using a blender, don't pack food into it. If a funnel cloud doesn't form, stop and stir. Or use a spatula to move the top layer, injecting air into the mixture.

Avocado Dressing

This was my mother's favorite dressing for fruit salad. I thought I had lost it years ago and struggled in vain to re-create it. Then, going through clippings for this cookbook—you guessed it, I found it! And the secret of its flavor is honey! Yes, you can use Buttermilk "Honey" (page 188).

3 apples, diced

4 tablespoons lemon juice, divided

1 cup buttermilk, well shaken

1 small ripe avocado, peeled, seeded, and cut into chunks

$\frac{1}{2}$ teaspoon lemon zest (approximate)

3 to 4 tablespoons honey

1 large orange, peeled, seeded, and sliced crosswise

$\frac{1}{4}$ cup raisins

$\frac{1}{2}$ cup unsalted cashews

Dice the apples and marinate in lemon juice to cover while you prepare the dressing.

For the dressing, combine the balance of the lemon juice, buttermilk, avocado, lemon zest, and honey in a blender. Process until smooth and thick.

Drain the apples and add the orange slices, raisins, and cashews. Combine with dressing and chill until ready to serve.

Yield: 2 cups

7 | *Main Dishes*

Southern Fried Chicken

Southern Fried Other Foods

Ultra-Tender Fried Chicken

Calves' Liver Stroganoff

Venison Stroganoff

Chicken Divan

Helen's Oven-Baked Chicken Casserole

Glazed Pork Roast

Beef Pot Roast

Salmon Pie with Artichoke Hearts

Salmon with Asparagus Tips

Leg of Lamb

Steak with Maître D'Hôtel Batter Butter

Beer-Battered Fish

Stuffed Flank Steak Baked in Buttermilk

Most of these recipes are for inexpensive (sometimes even cheap) cuts of meat. That's because one of buttermilk's many unheralded characteristics is its acidity. The lactic acid breaks down the cartilage of meat, tenderizing it as an elaborate marinade would. However, because of the milk solids in buttermilk, the sharpness and vinegarness usually associated with marinades are not present. The meat taste is not overwhelmed.

By the way, the use of buttermilk to tenderize meat has long been known by the same cooks who rely on buttermilk to make their biscuits better. I refer to those connoisseurs of fried chicken whose cornbread is sweeter, mashed potatoes fluffier, use of buttermilk greater than anyone else's.

They are also the ones who decided that milk-based—read buttermilk-based—gravies are fit and proper for any kind of meat, even chicken-fried steak.

Southern Fried Chicken

To many cooks, buttermilk-dipped fried chicken is the standard against which all other fried chicken recipes should be measured: It is simple. It has the lowest possible cholesterol. It has a slightly tangy taste as compared to the eggy taste that one sometimes experiences. It is simple—I said that before—but simple and not messy are in this case synonymous. And, buttermilk makes chicken better because it tenderizes it!

> **Cooking oil**
> **6 to 8 chicken pieces (about 2 pounds)**
> **1 cup flour**
> **¹/₂ teaspoon salt**
> **¹/₄ teaspoon pepper**
> **¹/₂ cup buttermilk**

Heat the oil, ³/₄ to 1 inch deep, in a frypan. Remove the chicken skin if you wish. If using legs, separate the thighs and drumsticks.

Dip the chicken pieces in the flour, seasoned with salt and pepper, then dip in buttermilk, and again in the flour. Fry in the oil almost to cover, without crowding.

Yield: 3 to 6 servings

Tips: Let the chicken sit for at least 10 minutes, preferably longer, after being coated and before cooking. This lets the coating settle and harden.

If I'm doing a large batch of chicken, I preheat the oven to 350° F. Fry the larger pieces of chicken first and, when well browned, move them to a rack in the cooking pan in the oven to finish cooking while doing the smaller pieces.

SOUTHERN FRIED OTHER FOODS
You can prepare pork chops, fish, chicken-fried steak—anything for which you normally use a flour-eggwash-flour dip.

ULTRA-TENDER FRIED CHICKEN
Marinate the chicken in buttermilk to cover for a minimum of 1 hour; I usually marinate for 8 hours or more. Instead of dipping the chicken twice in the flour, take the chicken pieces directly from the marinade and dip in the seasoned flour. Then fry.

Calves' Liver Stroganoff

Generally my family hates liver. But we like this dish—no strong liver taste or af-
tertaste. It is very colorful, especially if the green peppers are just barely cooked and
remain green. It can be made at the last minute or reheated. Serve with noodles.

4 slices calves' liver, ⅓ to ½ inch thick, cut into
   ⅓- to ½-inch-wide strips
1½ cups buttermilk
6 slices bacon
2 small onions, diced (about ½ cup)
1 green pepper, chopped coarsely (about ½ cup)
3 garlic cloves, minced
½ pound mushrooms, sliced (optional)
½ cup flour
½ teaspoon dry mustard
1 teaspoon salt
¼ teaspoon pepper
Oil (optional)
¼ cup white wine (optional)

The day before serving, place the sliced calves' liver in a flat container with enough buttermilk to cover. Cover with plastic wrap and refrigerate, turning the liver several times.
Sauté the bacon in a large frypan (don't microwave—you need to reserve the bacon fat)
and remove the bacon to paper towels to drain. Sauté the vegetables in the bacon fat until soft. Remove and keep warm.

Mix the dry ingredients together in a flat dish and reserve 2 tablespoons. Remove the
liver from the marinade—no need to pat dry—and dredge in the flour mixture. Add oil,
if necessary, to the bacon fat, to cover the bottom of the frypan. With heat turned up
high, quickly brown the liver on all sides. Do not overcook: Liver should be fork-tender.
Remove the liver to a dish with the vegetables and keep warm. Turn down heat and, if
desired, deglaze frypan with wine. Add the 2 tablespoons of reserved flour mixture to
the fat in the pan to make a roux. Add ½ cup buttermilk and cook until thick as gravy

(thin with more buttermilk if necessary). Taste and correct seasonings. Return vegetables and liver to the pan. Toss well. Serve with bacon crumbled on top.

Yield: 4 servings for liver lovers, 6 for others

Tip: Here's a place a where hand-held food processor comes in handy to dice, mince, and chop all the vegetables.

VENISON STROGANOFF

Prepare as for liver, using tender portions of venison cut into strips. You should have 2 cups' worth.

Chicken Divan

This is one of those recipes women love to serve to and share with other women.
An excellent buffet dish or luncheon dish.

4 whole chicken breasts, split and boned
2 boxes frozen broccoli spears
$\frac{1}{2}$ pound fresh mushrooms, sliced
2 tablespoons butter
2 tablespoons flour
1 cup buttermilk, at room temperature
1 can (10 $\frac{3}{4}$ ounces) condensed cream of mushroom soup

Preheat the oven to 350° F.

You will need a rectangular casserole, approximately 8 by 12 inches, plus two pans, one covered and large enough to hold the chicken breasts in one layer and one medium-size frypan. If you have purchased whole breasts, split and bone them.

In the larger pan, cover the bottom with water and arrange the chicken breasts, touching as little as possible. Cover and steam the breasts until they turn white and become firm, renewing water as needed. Remove the breasts to the rectangular casserole. Replace with the broccoli spears, adding additional water if necessary. Steam until the spears can be separated, remove and drain well. In a separate frypan, sauté the mushrooms in butter. When soft, remove the mushrooms with a slotted spoon to the casserole. Add the flour to the liquid in the frypan, mixing together to form a roux. Add the buttermilk and cook over low heat until slightly thickened. Add the soup and mix well. Pour over the layered chicken-broccoli-mushroom casserole.

Bake for 45 minutes, or until the chicken is fork-tender.

Yield: 4 large or 8 small portions

Tip: It is important that the buttermilk is at room temperature to begin with and cooked over low heat during thickening, otherwise it may curdle.

Helen's Oven-Baked Chicken Casserole

A so simple but so delicious dish that everyone who tastes it believes you slaved over it. It's a great entertaining dish because you can assemble it in less than fif-teen minutes, stick it in the oven several hours before serving, and let it make its own gravy.

1 package onion soup mix

6 chicken half breasts or 8 chicken thighs

1 can (10 ¾ ounces) condensed cream of mushroom soup

1 can measure of buttermilk

¼ cup sherry (optional)

You will need a 7 x 10-inch baking dish. Preheat the oven to 275° F (250° F if using a glass dish).

Remove the skin and excess fat from the chicken. Sprinkle the onion soup mix on the bottom of the baking dish. Place the pieces of chicken closely together atop the mix—they'll shrink during cooking. Dilute the soup with an equal amount of butter-milk; it will be thick. Add the sherry to the soup-buttermilk mixture if you wish. Pour and/or spread over the chicken.

Bake for 2½ to 3 hours, depending on the size of the chicken pieces. You may need to baste once after 2 hours if the tops of the chicken pieces become exposed.

Yield: 4 to 6 servings

Tip: Serve with rice, noodles, or mashed potatoes. There will be a lot of delicious, no-need-to-thicken gravy in the pan.

Glazed Pork Roast

I was so glad when lean pork came on the market as the "other white meat." My husband would gladly forgo steaks forever if he could have pork in some form once a week. This particular roast is special because it is made of a lower-cost meat, which buttermilk helps tenderize.

2 garlic cloves, crushed

2 medium yellow onions, sliced

6 medium carrots, cut into 1-inch chunks

2 tablespoons oil or margarine

3- to 4-pound boneless pork roast (butt or shoulder)

2 cups buttermilk

2 tablespoons cider vinegar

8 small potatoes

One 14-ounce can small white onions, or 16 fresh peeled

1 teaspoon salt

$\frac{1}{2}$ teaspoon pepper

2 tablespoons flour

Heat the oil or margarine in a heavy Dutch oven or large frying pan with cover. Brown the meat on all sides in the oil, then pour off the accumulated fat.

Reduce the heat to a simmer and add the buttermilk, vinegar, garlic, and sliced yellow onions. Cover and simmer over low heat until the pork is almost done. Add the carrots, potatoes, and small white onions, cover, and cook until the pork and vegetables are tender, about 20 minutes. Remove the pork to a platter and surround with the vegetables. Use the flour to make a gravy, adding additional water, if necessary.

Yield: 8 servings

Tips: To make a low-fat, low-calorie gravy, process the vegetables in a food processor, strain if desired, and bring to the right consistency by moistening with skimmed drippings.

BEEF POT ROAST

Do exactly the same thing, but use a solid piece of chuck roast.

Salmon Pie with Artichoke Hearts

This is simple but special. The tang of the buttermilk both emphasizes the flavor of the artichokes and salmon and blends them together. And this is one of those zip-together meals, the makings of which should be in everyone's pantry.

One 14-ounce can artichoke hearts
1 to 2 tablespoons butter or margarine
2 cups canned salmon (approximate)
Salt and pepper
½ cup cottage cheese
½ cup buttermilk
Sliced lemons for garnish

Preheat the oven to 375° F (350° F if using a glass dish). Sauté the artichoke hearts in butter until lightly browned. Butter a shallow baking dish.

Cover the bottom of the baking dish with the artichoke hearts. Flake the salmon and taste before adding salt and pepper. Pile on top of the artichoke hearts. Combine the cottage cheese and buttermilk and beat until smooth. Pour over the fish.

Bake for 20 minutes or longer until the topping is lightly browned. Serve with sliced lemons.

Yield: 6 servings

Tip: To make this dish a little piquant, add ½ to 1 teaspoon dry mustard to the cottage cheese–buttermilk mixture.

SALMON WITH ASPARAGUS TIPS

Substitute asparagus tips for the artichoke hearts. You may want to use individual ramekins, as asparagus is more likely to fall apart when served in a casserole. You can use fresh, canned, or leftover asparagus.

Leg of Lamb

There are times when it's a tough call to distinguish between lamb and mutton. Whenever I decide to serve a big leg of lamb, I take precautions to rid myself of that mutton taste. I marinate the meat in buttermilk—not for hours, but for days!

1 leg of lamb (8 to 9 pounds)
4 cups buttermilk (or more, as needed)
1 teaspoon salt
½ teaspoon pepper
12 to 15 whole cloves (optional)
1 large onion, sliced

Three days before serving, place the lamb in an enamel pan or glass bowl and cover with the buttermilk. Cover and refrigerate for 3 days, turning the lamb every morning and night.

Preheat the oven to 300° F. Remove the lamb from the buttermilk (reserving the buttermilk), blot dry with paper towels, rub with salt and pepper, and dot with cloves, if desired. Place on a rack in a roasting pan. Add the sliced onion and 1 cup of the buttermilk marinade to the pan.

Bake for 30 to 35 minutes per pound for medium lamb, less for rare. Baste every 20 minutes with the pan liquids or additional buttermilk, if needed.

Serve plain or with pan drippings gravy.

To make the gravy, skim off as much of the fat as possible. Combine 3 tablespoons cold water and 3 tablespoons all-purpose flour, rubbing until smooth. Dilute with an additional ¾ cup water, then slowly pour into the roasting pan. Stir until thickened.

Yield: 8 to 10 servings

Tip: Use 1 cup reserved buttermilk marinade to make the gravy: It will more closely resemble a sauce. If you don't like cloves, eliminate them, or if you want to be extra fancy, replace with juniper berries.

Steak with Maître D'Hôtel Batter Butter

When you want something guaranteed to please—everybody eats red meat once in a while—but still want to leave the impression that you've slaved for hours, serve steak with a very fancy but easy variation on Batter Butter. Prepare the steak your way.

1 teaspoon finely chopped shallot

¼ teaspoon finely chopped garlic

1 tablespoon finely chopped fresh parsley leaves

½ cup Batter Butter (page 25), at room temperature

¾ tablespoon lemon juice

½ teaspoon salt, or to taste

¼ teaspoon freshly ground pepper

Cream the Batter Butter and add the remaining ingredients, mixing until well blended. Prepare ahead of time and store in the refrigerator.

Use a melon cutter to make balls out of Batter Butter for presentation on steaks. Do it at the very last minute, or serve the balls separately on a dish of ice.

Tip: If you want to make it faster, do everything—including chopping—in a mini–food processor. You'll need 1 shallot, 1 very small garlic clove, and a bunch of parsley about 1½ inches across the top.

Beer-Battered Fish

This is nothing more than an Americanized version of tempura. Use cod or cat-fish, jack salmon, bluefish, monkfish, bass—whatever's the catch of the day. Don't confine yourself to fish—use chicken, shrimp, or onion rings.

2 to 3 cups vegetable oil

1 cup Buttermilk Baking Mix (page 180)

¼ teaspoon pepper

Garlic salt (optional)

Salt (optional)

1 cup beer

**2 to 3 pounds fish fillets, cleaned and cut into small- or
     medium-size pieces**

Heat the vegetable oil to 375° F in a skillet.

Combine the baking mix and pepper and salts, if using, and the beer—slowly. Dry fish fillets thoroughly, then dip in the batter.

Fry a few pieces at a time in the hot oil until golden brown. Drain on a rack or on absorbent paper towels.

Yield: 4 to 6 servings

Tip: Whether or not you use salt depends on the pancake mix you use. If it's homemade with salt, you shouldn't need additional salt. If it's salt-free homemade or commercial, you will.

Stuffed Flank Steak Baked in Buttermilk

I usually marinate the flank steak first in buttermilk to help tenderize it, depending on is quality. I then use the marinade in cooking the meat roll.

2½ cups soft bread crumbs

⅓ cup butter, melted

1 teaspoon chopped onion

1 teaspoon salt

Dash of pepper

1 flank steak

2 to 3 tablespoons margarine, oil, or butter

2 cups buttermilk

Water

¼ cup flour

Preheat the oven to 350° F (325° F if using a glass dish).

Mix the bread crumbs, butter, onion, ½ teaspoon of the salt, and the pepper. Spread over the steak and roll up. Tuck in the ends, tie with string or fasten with skewers. Season with the remaining salt. In a large skillet, brown the meat on all sides in butter. Transfer to a baking dish, add the buttermilk, and cover.

Bake for 1 hour and 30 minutes or until tender. Remove the roll from the pan and keep warm.

Mash and pour the drippings through a sieve into a deep saucepan. Add water to the flour and mix to a paste. Cook, stirring constantly, until thickened. If necessary, add more buttermilk or more water. Pour the gravy over the meat or pass separately.

Yield: 6 servings

Tip: To give an essentially bland stuffing some zip, add some chopped parsley and/or ½ teaspoon sage.

For a change from traditional stuffing, use commercial, thin slices of ham instead of the bread-onion-butter mixture.

8 | *Vegetables*

Savory Corn Bake

Bacon Savory Corn Bake

Vegetables au Gratin

Green Beans and Almonds

Broccoli and/or Cauliflower

Baby Carrots and Onions

Potatoes

Rice and Chile Pepper Casserole

Vegetable Hash Casserole

Buttermilk Mashed Potatoes

Garlic Mashed Potatoes

Instant Mashed Potatoes

Batter-Fried Onion Rings

Batter-Fried Vegetables

Buttered Vegetables

Lemon Butter

Savory Mustard Butter

No-Work Mustard Butter

To tell the truth, other than in vegetable casseroles, I don't use much buttermilk in conjunction with vegetables. However, there are exceptions. I like to add a dollop or two of buttermilk to the cooking water when doing any vegetable whose color might change during the cooking. It is especially good with cauliflower. You may already be doing the same thing with vinegar or lemon. The difference is that the acid in buttermilk helps retain color, but its flavor dissipates, while vinegar or lemon leave a lingering taste.

Also, I absolutely adore baked potatoes slathered with Batter Butter (plus a judicious amount of salt and pepper). It tastes a little like a tangy butter, a little like a buttery sour cream, and a lot like something out of this world.

A white or cheese sauce made with buttermilk will look rich and have great mouth appeal but will have nowhere near the calories you might expect. If you're trying to keep the calories way down, make it with Batter Butter. Use the same quantities and proportions as usual, but be sure to whisk in the flour completely before adding the liquid. I frequently make mine with Batter Butter, flour, nonfat dried milk powder, and boiling water. Not only is it low cal but it goes together fast.

Savory Corn Bake

This is a dish I like to serve at buffets and family gatherings, but it's also a terrific luncheon or Sunday night supper dish. It's a combination corn pudding, Spanish omelet, and spoon bread. In other words, a meal in a bowl!

2 eggs, separated

1 cup buttermilk

½ cup stirred, scooped, and leveled flour

2 tablespoons cornmeal

1 teaspoon salt, or to taste

⅛ teaspoon pepper

½ teaspoon baking soda

1 teaspoon baking powder

One 16-ounce can cream-style corn

½ cup chopped green pepper

1 cup diced cooked ham

½ cup diced onion (optional)

Preheat the oven to 350° F (325° F if using a glass baking dish). Grease a 2-quart casserole. Just before you begin preparation, beat the egg whites until stiff but not dry.

Beat the egg yolks with the buttermilk in a large mixing bowl. Add the dry ingredients and beat until smooth. Add the corn, green pepper, ham, and onion, if using. Fold in the egg whites. Turn the mixture into the casserole dish.

Bake for about 1 hour or until the top is golden brown.

This dish does not freeze well, but have no fear—none will be left over.

Yield: 4 to 6 servings

BACON SAVORY CORN BAKE

Replace the ham with ½ pound bacon, fried, drained, and crumbled.

Tip: Use your microwave to cook the bacon until crisp. Don't undercook it, thinking it will cook more while in the oven—it won't.

Vegetables au Gratin

An excellent buffet dish that can be made from almost any vegetable or combi-nation of vegetables. The low-fat buttermilk offsets the fat grams in the cheese. Make it ahead of time, refrigerate, and cook at the last minute.

1½ cups buttermilk, at room temperature

3 cups fresh or frozen vegetables, such as green beans,
    sliced thin

½ cup processed American cheese, diced or grated

Parmesan cheese, grated

4 tablespoons butter or margarine

4 tablespoons flour

1 teaspoon salt

⅛ teaspoon dry mustard

Paprika

Cook the vegetables in salted boiling water until partially done (blanched). Butter a 1½-quart casserole dish. Preheat the oven to 350° F (325° F if using a glass dish). Dice or grate the processed cheese and grate the Parmesan.

Prepare the cheese sauce by melting the butter in a saucepan. Add the flour, salt, and mustard. Cook over low heat until the mixture bubbles. Remove from the heat and stir vigorously as you add the buttermilk, to keep it from curdling. Return to the heat and cook until thick and smooth. Add the cheese and stir until melted. Add the vegetables and pour into the casserole. Sprinkle with Parmesan (if freshly grated, you can't add too much—at least half of a small wedge). Dust with paprika.

Bake for 30 minutes until bubbly.

Yield: 6 servings

GREEN BEANS AND ALMONDS
Add one 3 to 4-ounce package slivered almonds with the Parmesan cheese.

BROCCOLI AND/OR CAULIFLOWER
Besides frozen or fresh vegetables, try this recipe with leftovers. No one will ever know.

BABY CARROTS AND ONIONS
Use equal amounts of canned carrots and onions.

POTATOES
Peel and slice thinly. Parboil in salted water for 10 minutes. Remove, drain, and pat dry. Put in casserole in layers, adding cheese sauce alternately.

Rice and Chile Pepper Casserole

What would a modern cookbook be without a recipe for something spicy? This is moderately so and will be moreso if you get any chile pepper seeds in it.

One 4-ounce can green chile peppers, seeded and chopped
³/₄ pound cheddar cheese, grated
1¹/₂ cups cottage cheese
1¹/₂ cups buttermilk
4 cups packed cooked rice
Salt and pepper

Preheat the oven to 350° F (325° F if using a glass dish). Grease a 1¹/₂-quart casserole.

Blend the cottage cheese and buttermilk, and mix with the peppers. Season the rice with salt and pepper. Layer the mixture, beginning with the rice, then the cottage-cheese/buttermilk, then the cheddar. Repeat so that you have six layers in all.

Bake until bubbly, about 25 minutes.

Yield: 6 servings

VEGETABLE HASH CASSEROLE
Instead of chiles, use chopped green and/or red peppers; ditto for onions that have been fried until softened. (If I have leftover corn, I'll add that, too.) Layer as above.

Buttermilk Mashed Potatoes

This is one of those recipes that suddenly and simultaneously is discovered by everyone. Anyone who's into reducing calories in mashed potatoes seems to have come up with the same brilliant idea of using buttermilk. Actually, a potato in itself is not high in calories—it's the butter, sour cream, cheese, bacon, all the good-tasting stuff we put on it. And I blame that on the potato industry. Potato farmers seem bound and determined to produce a nontasting potato to match the nontasting tomatoes we were plagued with for years. A homegrown potato, baked, salted, and peppered, can be as good eating as you might wish. And for a low-calorie storebought potato, I recommend topping it with Batter Butter in place of butter and sour cream.

However, if you're in the mood for mashed potatoes and feel your potatoes need flavor-doctoring, here's how.

1 pound (4 medium) white potatoes

1½ teaspoons salt

¾ cup warm buttermilk

½ teaspoon baking soda

2 teaspoons unsalted butter or Batter Butter (page 25), or
    more as needed

Freshly ground pepper

Scrub and peel the potatoes, if you wish. Place the potatoes in a saucepan with water to cover and 1 teaspoon salt. Bring to a boil over high heat. Reduce the heat and simmer until the potatoes are tender when pierced with a fork. Drain potatoes.

Place the potatoes back in the pan over heat and shake until they are dry. Mash with a fork or potato masher until fairly smooth (some lumps can remain). Combine the warm buttermilk and baking soda and beat into the potatoes with a spoon. Add the butter and remaining salt and pepper to taste.

Yield: 4 servings

Tip: This is one place an electric mixer will let you down. It can turn mashed potatoes into potato paste. However, a hand-held food processor works well.

GARLIC MASHED POTATOES

If you really like garlic, you'll like these. Add 5 whole garlic cloves to the potatoes during cooking. Mash the garlic with the potatoes.

INSTANT MASHED POTATOES

If you're into instant, try using buttermilk instead of whole milk.

Batter-Fried Onion Rings

I wish I could say this recipe is totally original; it's not. It is adapted from a recipe of James Beard's that he credits to Cecily Brownstone of the Associated Press.

2 to 3 large sweet onions
Vegetable oil for frying
1 egg
1 cup buttermilk
1 cup stirred, scooped, and leveled all-purpose flour
³/₄ teaspoon salt
¹/₂ teaspoon baking soda
¹/₂ teaspoon white pepper or cayenne pepper, or to taste

Peel and slice the onions into ¹/₄-inch-thick slices and separate into rings. Soak in ice water for 2 hours, adding more ice if necessary. Drain thoroughly. Return to the refrigerator to rechill.

Preheat the oil to 375° F.

Make the batter by beating the egg and buttermilk together and stir in the dry ingredients. Remove the onion rings from the refrigerator and dip in the batter a few at a time; fry in small batches. Remove from the fat when browned and drain on absorbent paper towels. Transfer to a cookie sheet in a preheated 325° F oven to keep warm until all are done.

Yield: 6 servings

Tips: If you're going to make a big batch, to guarantee the batter doesn't go flat, use ¼ teaspoon baking powder instead of ½ teaspoon baking soda.

You can use homemade Buttermilk Baking Mix (page 180) for this recipe if you thin down the batter. I do so by eliminating the liquid buttermilk and adding beer, which adds extra leavening.

You can use any vegetable—including broccoli, mushrooms, eggplant, or zucchini—cut into finger-size pieces.

Buttered Vegetables

A recipe for such a simple thing? I know, you just take a gob and put it on your potato or your green beans. But that gob, if it's real butter, is high in fat and can be almost as high if it's margarine. So what to do? Use Batter Butter. You can also add some extra-special seasonings.

LEMON BUTTER

¼ cup Batter Butter (page 25)
1 to 2 tablespoons chopped parsley
1 tablespoon lemon juice

To soften the Batter Butter, add the parsley and lemon juice. Mix and serve over vegetables.

Yield: ⅓ cup

Tip: Lemon butter is good with steak or fish, too. I particularly like it with veal or with plain noodles.

SAVORY MUSTARD BUTTER

½ cup Batter Butter (page 25)

2 tablespoons Dijon mustard

2 tablespoons capers, drained and chopped fine

½ teaspoon coarsely ground pepper

Salt

Mix all the ingredients together until well blended and fluffy.

Yield: Approximately ½ to ¾ cup

NO-WORK MUSTARD BUTTER

Add 2 teaspoons prepared mustard to ½ cup Batter Butter.

9 | *Desserts*

Buttermilk Velvet

> *Chunky Fruit Pudding*

> *Berry Special*

> *Basically Perfect*

Spa Sherbet

> *Strawberry Sherbet*

> *Peach Sherbet*

> *Banana Sherbet*

> *Avocado Sherbet*

Berry Sherbet

> *Fruit Sherbet*

> *Banana Sliced Sherbet*

> *Pineapple Sherbet*

Orange Mousse

> *Lemon or Lime Mousse*

Chocolate Frozen Soufflé

Hot Chocolate Soufflé

Chocolate Mint Soufflé

Mocha Soufflé

Coffee Soufflé

Grand Marnier Soufflé

Low-Fat Hot Orange Soufflé

Danish Sweet Buttermilk "Soup"

Dessert "Soup"

Rice Pudding

Blueberry Grunt

Applesauce Grunt

Gingerbread with Lemon Sauce

Orange Sauce

Cherry Cobbler

Peach Cobbler

Brownie Pudding

Raisin Bread Pudding

Chocolate Bread Pudding

Egg Nog Pudding

Lemon Sponge Pudding

Pecan-Molasses Supreme

Crème Fraîche

Desserts, I love 'em—they love me too much. What did the wit say? Desserts give you all the fat that's fit to wear. In truth, those calories cling to my waist, my hips, my everywhere more easily than Velcro. I should hate to add up the number of days of dieting I've done in the past because of my inordinate fondness for desserts. But—and this is the good part—that was in the past, before I began working with buttermilk. Now I enjoy, fat free and guilt free—and I hope you will, too.

Why does buttermilk make a difference? The low calories, the low cholesterol, the low fat. But other products have that too, so what makes buttermilk special? The milk solids and emulsifiers contained therein.

If you like yogurt desserts, you should appreciate buttermilk ones. And if you don't like buttermilk, you'll still like these desserts—I know because that describes me perfectly.

And if you ask my opinion, the very first dessert in this chapter is worth the price of the book. It has the mouth appeal and apparent richness of whipped cream, but not the sweetness or the fat.

Buttermilk Velvet

As my husband says, this one's a winner. It has everything going for it. It's simple to make. It's voluptuously rich. It's the dieter's friend: low-calorie (fewer than 100 calories per serving), low-fat (3 grams per servings), low everything, except taste!

One 8-ounce carton frozen light whipped topping
1 cup buttermilk
One 1-ounce package instant fat-free, sugar-free vanilla
   pudding mix

If the whipped topping is hard-frozen, let it thaw.

Combine the whipped topping and the buttermilk and stir in the instant pudding mix. Spoon into individual dishes, cover and refrigerate until ready to serve.

Yield: 8 servings

Tip: It is best to mix with a whisk or spoon, not a mixer.

If you've watched your calories all day, reward yourself with a sprinkling of cookie crumbs on top.

You can double it, halve it, make it in advance, and refrigerate it. You can freeze it. What you can't do is resist it!

CHUNKY FRUIT PUDDING
Use 32 ounces of canned fruit in light syrup, well drained. You can use fruit salad, canned peaches, mandarin oranges with crushed pineapple. The only criteria is that the fruit be well drained.

BERRY SPECIAL
Thaw and drain frozen fruit—raspberries, strawberries, blueberries—or use fresh fruit. Use one package/pint, except on special occasions when you can double that amount. Serve chilled or freeze. Let soften slightly before serving.

BASICALLY PERFECT
Use chocolate, butterscotch, or any other flavor of instant pudding and freeze for a dessert better and no less tangy than any frozen yogurt on the market.

Spa Sherbet

Historically, this has been called a sherbet; technically, it's an ice milk. In either case, for decades it's been the low-fat dessert of choice among guests spending thousands of dollars per week at slenderizing spas in Arizona and Texas.

1 quart buttermilk

³/₄ cup fresh-squeezed or reconstituted lemon juice

1 cup light corn syrup

6 tablespoons grated lemon peel

1 cup sugar or artificial sweetener, or to taste

Ready an ice cream machine according to the manufacturer's directions, or, for still-freezing, use two nonpartitioned ice-cube trays or metal loaf pans.

Combine all the ingredients in a large saucepan over low heat, stirring until the sugar is dissolved. If using artificial sweetener, simply combine the ingredients well but do not heat.

Freeze according to the machine's directions. Or still-freeze by pouring into metal trays three-quarters full and cover with foil. Freeze until mushy. Beat in a mixing bowl until smooth and return to original trays. Freeze until firm.

Do not double this recipe. Remove from the freezer to refrigerator about 15 minutes before serving.

Yield: 1 quart

Tip: For coarse-grained granita-like sherbet, scrape slush in trays—from front to back—every 30 minutes until sherbert has frozen solid.

STRAWBERRY SHERBET
Add 1 cup pureed strawberries to mixture and reduce lemon juice to ¹/₄ cup.

PEACH SHERBET
Add 1 cup pureed peaches, either canned or very ripe, and reduce lemon juice to ¹/₄ cup.

BANANA SHERBET

Reduce lemon juice to 1 tablespoon and add 2 medium-size bananas, mashed.

AVOCADO SHERBET

Only the use of buttermilk keeps this sherbet even semihealthy since avocados are so high in fat. However, between the avocado and the buttermilk, they balance out. Add 2 cups pureed avocado to the mixture; you can replace the lemon juice with lime juice.

Berry Sherbet

The difference between this and the previous recipe is the gelatin, which means the mixture will thicken easier. As for taste, they're both very good, especially when they're so low in fat and calories.

2 cups frozen berries
1/4 cup sugar (optional)
1 envelope unflavored gelatin
1 1/2 cups buttermilk
1/2 cup sugar
2 tablespoons lemon juice

Ready an ice cream machine according to the manufacturer's directions, or, for still-freezing, use two nonpartitioned ice-cube trays or metal loaf pans. Defrost the berries, mash and drain, reserving 1/3 cup juice. If berries are unsweetened, add the 1/4 cup sugar, if desired.

In a small saucepan, combine the gelatin with the reserved 1/3 cup juice, add 1/2 cup of the buttermilk, and heat just until the gelatin is dissolved. Remove from heat, add the sugar and stir well, then add the balance of the buttermilk, berries, and lemon juice.

Freeze according to the machine's directions. Or still-freeze by pouring into two trays or pans and freezing until mushy. Beat in a mixing bowl until smooth and return to original trays. Freeze until firm.

Yield: 6 to 8 servings

Tip: If using fresh berries, mash with 1/4 cup sugar and allow to drain—this will take about 10 minutes. Reserve 1/3 cup juice.

FRUIT SHERBET

Besides any frozen fruit—strawberries, raspberries, blueberries—you can use fresh or canned peaches, apricots, or pears. If unsweetened or non-sugar packed, add ¼ cup sugar. (Please note: Melon balls do not work satisfactorily as their natural flavor is too delicate to stand up under freezing. You must reinforce with artificial flavor.)

SLICED-BANANA SHERBET

After the first freezing, add sliced bananas to the mixture. Complete the recipe as instructed.

PINEAPPLE SHERBET

Increase the sugar to ¾ cup and use a 9-ounce can crushed pineapple (drained, reserving ⅓ cup juice) instead of berries. Just before freezing, fold in 1 stiffly beaten egg white and 1 teaspoon vanilla. Freeze, stir, and refreeze.

Orange Mousse

The name is sort of a put-off—it sounds French-fancy, but it's not. It requires no special equipment or long cooking time. The combination of gelatin and egg whites guarantees a very light, delicate dessert. If I had my druthers, I'd much rather make and serve a mousse than an ice cream.

4 eggs

1 tablespoon unflavored gelatin

¼ cup cold water

2 cups buttermilk

½ cup sugar or artificial sweetener, or to taste

½ cup orange juice

2 tablespoons grated orange zest

Separate the eggs while still cold. Soften the gelatin in the cold water, about 5 minutes.

Combine the egg yolks, buttermilk, and sugar in a saucepan over low heat. Cook, stirring frequently, until thick and the mixture coats a spoon. Remove from heat and add the gelatin, orange juice, and orange peel. Let cool in the refrigerator until the mixture begins to congeal. Beat the egg whites until stiff and fold into the mixture. Spoon the mixture into a soufflé dish and refrigerate until ready to serve.

Yield: 4 generous servings or 6 small servings

Tip: Before folding in the beaten egg whites, first stir 1 large spoonful of whites into the mixture to lighten it. Then fold in the balance. For an extra-light mousse, you can use up to twice as many egg whites.

Do not double the recipe.

This mousse also freezes well.

LEMON OR LIME MOUSSE

Replace the orange juice and peel, ounce for ounce and tablespoon for tablespoon, with lemon or lime. Before refrigerating, taste the cooked mixture for sweetness. You may wish to add more sugar. Serve with a garnish of apricot halves, if desired.

Chocolate Frozen Soufflé

Do you like frozen yogurt? You'll like this.

1 envelope unflavored gelatin

¼ cup cold water

2 squares (2 ounces) unsweetened chocolate, melted

½ cup confectioners' sugar

¾ cup sugar

1 cup buttermilk

1 teaspoon vanilla extract

⅛ teaspoon (pinch) salt

2 cups heavy cream, whipped, or whipped topping

You will need a large freezer-proof mixing bowl, small saucepan, and 5-cup serving dish, chilled. If using heavy cream, chill the mixer bowl and beaters. Soften the gelatin in the cold water.

Melt the chocolate in a small saucepan over *very* low heat and stir in the confectioners' sugar. Add the softened gelatin and stir until dissolved. Add the sugar and buttermilk and stir until the sugar is dissolved. Remove from the heat, transfer to a large mixing bowl, add the vanilla, and chill just until the mixture begins to set. Fold in the whipped cream or whipped topping and transfer the mixture to the chilled serving dish. Chill—do not freeze—for 6 hours or until thoroughly set. Serve directly from the bowl.

Yield: 6 servings

Tip: If whipping heavy cream, add the vanilla just as the beaters begin to make a definite wavy pattern.

Hot Chocolate Soufflé

One of two hot soufflés that benefit from buttermilk. In this case, buttermilk gives the chocolate a tang very reminiscent of a devil's food cake.

1 package (6 ounces) semisweet chocolate bits

3 tablespoons butter or margarine, plus more as needed

3 tablespoons flour

1 cup buttermilk

⅓ cup sugar, plus more as needed

⅛ teaspoon (pinch) salt

4 eggs, separated

1 teaspoon vanilla extract

Thoroughly butter and sugar a 6-cup ovenproof soufflé dish, knocking out any excess sugar. Preheat the oven to 350° F and remove all but the bottom rack. Melt the chocolate bits in the microwave in 30-second bursts or in a small saucepan over *very* low heat.

Melt the butter in a large saucepan over medium heat. Add the flour and mix thoroughly. Gradually add the buttermilk and stir constantly until the mixture is thick. Remove the pan from the heat and add the sugar and salt. Stir in the melted chocolate.

In a large electric mixer bowl, beat the egg yolks until thick. Then gradually add the hot mixture to the egg yolks, beating constantly. Add the vanilla. Set the mixture aside to cool, stirring occasionally. (Stir more frequently if you put the mixing bowl in cold water or over ice cubes.) The recipe can be made ahead to this point.

With clean beaters and using a small bowl, beat the egg whites until stiff but not dry.

When the egg yolk mixture has cooled to a lukewarm temperature, stir in one large spoonful of egg whites to lighten the base. Fold in the balance of the egg whites, and *gently* transfer the mixture to the prepared dish.

Optional: To make a "top hat," remove about ½ inch of the soufflé mixture from the edge by running (or gouging) your thumb around it, piling the excess mixture into the middle.

Bake for 30 minutes for a firm soufflé. (If you like your soufflé soft in the middle, bake 20 to 25 minutes in a 375° F oven.) Serve *immediately*. Use a fork to break through the crust.

Yield: 4 to 6 servings

Tip: Add ¼ teaspoon baking soda to the egg yolk mixture before adding the egg whites. The combination of baking soda and buttermilk guarantees that the soufflé will rise— and stay that way a precious few minutes longer.

CHOCOLATE MINT SOUFFLÉ

Add ¼ cup white crème de menthe in place of vanilla.

MOCHA SOUFFLÉ

Add 2 tablespoons instant coffee to the melted chocolate.

COFFEE SOUFFLÉ

Add 2 tablespoons instant coffee and eliminate the melted chocolate.

GRAND MARNIER SOUFFLÉ

Reduce the amount of buttermilk to ¾ cup. Add the grated peel of 1 orange and add ⅓ cup Grand Marnier instead of the vanilla.

Low-Fat Hot Orange Soufflé

Did I say low fat? I could have said practically fat-free. It has but one milligram of cholesterol per serving too. Yet it's rich tasting and easy to make. I have SACO Foods to thank for this recipe.

2 tablespoons cornstarch

2 tablespoons sugar

3 tablespoons dried cultured buttermilk

¾ cup water

3 tablespoons frozen orange juice concentrate, thawed

2 tablespoons low-sugar orange marmalade

1 teaspoon vanilla extract

5 egg whites, at room temperature

½ teaspoon cream of tartar

Preheat the oven to 425° F. Spray the bottom of a 2-quart soufflé dish with nonstick cooking spray.

Combine the dry ingredients in a medium-size nonaluminum saucepan. Add the water, orange juice, and marmalade. Cook over medium heat until thickened, stirring constantly. Pour into a large bowl, add vanilla, and let cool to room temperature. In a small mixer bowl, beat the egg whites and cream of tartar at high speed with an electric mixer until stiff but not dry. Fold in the egg whites. Spoon the mixture into the prepared soufflé dish.

Bake for 1 minute. Reduce heat to 375° F and bake an additional 20 to 25 minutes until puffy and golden brown. Serve immediately.

Yield: 6 servings

Tip: Lighten the creamed sauce by mixing in 1 very large spoonful of egg whites and incorporate gently before folding in the balance of egg whites.

Danish Sweet Buttermilk "Soup"

To call this a "soup" is almost as much a misnomer as "buttermilk" itself. It is actually a soupy, custardy rice pudding. Try it for dessert after a light meal, accompanied by sturdy English biscuits or cookies. Or do as the Danes do (they have their big meal at lunch) and serve it as an entrée-dessert for a Sunday or late-evening supper. One of the national dishes of Denmark, it is somewhat reminiscent of the Greek avgolemono soup. The contrast between the hot and the cold, the tart and the sweet, make this a truly different dessert soup.

½ cup enriched (not instant) long-grain rice

8 cups buttermilk

Rind of 1 lemon, grated

One 2- to 3-inch cinnamon stick

⅓ cup raisins

2 egg yolks

2 tablespoons sugar

1 cup whipped and lightly sweetened heavy cream, or
    whipped topping

Slivered or chopped almonds

Chop the rice in a blender for 30 seconds or until the grains are the size of kosher salt.

In a 3-quart saucepan, combine the rice, buttermilk, lemon rind, cinnamon stick, and raisins. Cook over low heat, stirring almost constantly to prevent curdling. (You may see some white flecks on top that look like curdled milk; don't worry, they'll disappear.) Cook for 45 to 55 minutes or until the mixture thickens and the rice is soft.

Beat the egg yolks with the sugar. Slowly add ½ cup of the hot soup to the yolks and mix well, then return the egg yolk mixture to the soup and continue cooking another 3 to 5 minutes until the mixture thickens considerably.

Top each serving of hot soup with a generous spoonful of chilled whipped cream and a sprinkling of almonds.

Yield: 8 servings

Tip: This soup is equally good cold, so make the entire recipe for two distinctive desserts.
    Do not double the recipe; it does not freeze well.

Dessert "Soup"

Another soup, but this one everybody likes since it's tapioca pudding going by its original centuries-old name. I think it works better with small-grained tapioca instead of the pearl ones.

2 cups water

4 cups buttermilk

¼ cup tapioca

½ cup raisins (optional)

1 or 2 sticks cinnamon

1 egg, well beaten

⅛ teaspoon salt

3 tablespoons sugar

In a large saucepan, bring water to a boil. Add the buttermilk slowly, stirring constantly until it boils. Add the tapioca, raisins (if using), and cinnamon sticks and keep stirring until it boils again. Reduce the heat and let simmer until the tapioca is cooked (it will appear clear). Remove from the heat; fish out the cinnamon sticks and discard.

Add the salt and sugar to the well-beaten egg, and then add a tablespoon at a time the ½ cup (approximately) of the hot mixture.

Return the egg mixture to the balance of the tapioca mixture and cook about ten minutes or until thickened.

Serve hot or cold.

Yield: 6 servings

RICE PUDDING
Replace the tapioca with an equal amount of long-grain rice.

Blueberry Grunt

An old-fashioned recipe that dates back to colonial days, but the methodology of its making remains the same: blueberries brought to a boil, and biscuit dough placed on top.

 4 pints fresh blueberries

 1 cup sugar

 1 tablespoon cornstarch

 1 teaspoon cinnamon (optional)

 1 tablespoon lemon juice

 Water to cover

 1 cup stirred, scooped, and leveled all-purpose flour

 1 teaspoon baking powder

 1/4 teaspoon baking soda

 1/8 teaspoon (pinch) salt

 2 tablespoons margarine, shortening, or butter, melted

 1/2 cup buttermilk, or more as needed

 Ice cream, whipped cream, or whipped topping (optional)

Use a large saucepan or skillet with a cover. (I use an electric one). Wash the blueberries and pick them over for stems, leaves, etc.

Place the blueberries in the pan, add the sugar, cornstarch, and cinnamon, if desired; stir to coat the blueberries, sprinkle with the lemon juice, and add water to cover. Bring to a gentle boil.

In a mixing bowl, add the flour, baking powder, baking soda, and salt, and stir well. Combine the melted shortening with the buttermilk and add to the dry ingredients, stirring quickly until moistened and a soft dough is formed.

Drop by large spoonfuls—work quickly—onto the boiling blueberry mixture. Cover the pan tightly, reduce heat until the mixture simmers, and cook for 15 minutes before lifting the lid. If the dumplings aren't done (test with a fork) continue cooking with the lid on.

Serve as is or with the optional ice cream, whipped cream, or whipped topping.

Yield: 6 to 8 servings

Tip: Better to undermix than overmix.

 This does not freeze well.

APPLESAUCE GRUNT

Use a large can of ready-made applesauce or apple pie filling instead of blueberries. You will have to make a judgment call as to how much water to add. The mixture should be runny enough so it won't burn during 15 minutes of gentle boiling—¼ to ½ cup should be sufficient. Be sure to taste the applesauce for sweetness. Add cinnamon and ¼ teaspoon nutmeg, if desired.

Gingerbread with Lemon Sauce

This dessert may be my all-time favorite. It brings back fond memories of Christmas and Thanksgiving and good times.

> 4 to 5 tablespoons butter, melted
>
> 1 cup sugar
>
> 2 tablespoons molasses
>
> 1 teaspoon salt
>
> 1 teaspoon cinnamon
>
> ½ teaspoon ground cloves
>
> ¼ teaspoon ginger
>
> 1 egg
>
> 2 cups stirred, scooped, and leveled all-purpose flour
>
> 1 teaspoon baking soda
>
> 1 cup buttermilk
>
> 1 tablespoon grated lemon zest (optional)

Preheat the oven to 400° F. Grease and flour an 8-inch-square baking pan.

Blend the butter with the sugar and molasses. Add the salt, cinnamon, cloves, and ginger and stir well. Beat in the egg. Mix the flour and baking soda together and add alternately with the buttermilk to the butter and sugar mixture, beginning and ending with the dry ingredients. Pour batter into the pan.

Bake for 35 minutes. After removing from the oven, let the pan sit on a rack for about 5 minutes before removing the gingerbread.

Yield: 6 or more servings

Tip: Best when served fresh and warm, especially with the warm lemon sauce.

LEMON SAUCE

¹/₂ cup sugar

1 tablespoon flour

1 tablespoon cornstarch

¹/₈ teaspoon (pinch) salt

¹/₈ teaspoon nutmeg

1 cup boiling water

2 tablespoons butter or margarine, cut into small pieces

1¹/₂ tablespoons lemon juice, fresh, frozen, or canned

1 teaspoon grated lemon zest

Combine the sugar, flour, cornstarch, salt, and nutmeg in a saucepan. Gradually blend in the water. Cook over low heat, stirring constantly until thick and clear, about 10 minutes. Add the butter, a few pieces at a time, until melted and incorporated. Remove from the heat. Add the lemon juice and zest and stir. Serve warm or cold.

Yield: 1¹/₃ cups

ORANGE SAUCE

Use the grated zest and juice of 1 orange as well as the juice of 1 lemon. Eliminate the lemon zest.

Cherry Cobbler

Although a cobbler and a grunt—strange names those—are essentially the same thing, there is a difference: in the dough. The grunt's dumplings are softer and doughier than the cobbler's more hearty crust baked on top.

FRUIT FILLING

2½ cups unsweetened, pitted cherries, canned or frozen

1 cup sugar

1 tablespoon tapioca

½ teaspoon vanilla extract

COBBLER

1½ cups stirred, scooped, and leveled all-purpose flour

2 teaspoons baking powder

¼ teaspoon baking soda

1 tablespoon sugar, plus more for garnish as needed

½ teaspoon salt

⅓ cup shortening or oil

½ cup buttermilk

1 egg, well beaten

Preheat the oven to 400° F. Grease an 8 x 8 x 2-inch square pan.

Mix the cherries, sugar, tapioca, and vanilla and pour into the pan. Keep cherry mixture warm in the oven while preparing the cobbler.

Stir together the flour, baking powder, baking soda, 1 tablespoon sugar, and salt. Cut in the shortening with a pastry blender or food processor until the mixture resembles little peas. Add the buttermilk and egg, stirring only until the flour is just moistened.

Spread the dough over the hot cherries. Sprinkle with additional sugar, if desired.

Bake for 35 to 40 minutes.

Yield: 8 servings

PEACH COBBLER

Use 3 cups sliced fresh peaches and add 1 tablespoon lemon juice and 1 teaspoon grated lemon zest to the fruit. Arrange the peaches in a pan. Combine the sugar, tapioca, and vanilla and sprinkle over the peaches. Continue as above.

Brownie Pudding

Think of everything you like about brownies: This dessert has them all. It's chocolaty, chewy, almost fudgy. It may not be death by chocolate, but young people think it's to die for.

1³/₄ cups hot water

1 cup stirred, scooped, and leveled all-purpose flour

1 teaspoon baking powder

¹/₄ teaspoon baking soda

³/₄ cup sugar

¹/₄ cup plus 2 tablespoons cocoa

¹/₂ teaspoon salt

¹/₂ cup buttermilk

1 teaspoon vanilla extract

2 tablespoons melted shortening or oil

³/₄ cup chopped walnuts

³/₄ cup brown sugar

Preheat the oven to 350° F. Grease an 8 x 8 x 2-inch square pan. Heat the water.

Combine the flour, baking powder, baking soda, sugar, 2 tablespoons of the cocoa, and salt. Add the buttermilk, vanilla, and shortening or oil. Mix until smooth and add the nuts. Pour the batter into the pan. Combine the brown sugar and ¹/₄ cup of the cocoa and sprinkle over the batter. Then pour the hot water slowly over the entire surface.

Bake for 40 to 45 minutes.

Yield: 6 or more servings

Tip: When pouring the water, do it quickly but not from too great a height above the batter.

Raisin Bread Pudding

This is very reminiscent of an old-fashioned steamed brown pudding. In fact, it was originally made with suet. You needn't steam it on the range though. Simply give it a water bath in the oven.

½ **cup margarine or butter**
½ **cup packed brown sugar**
3 **cups unseasoned bread crumbs**
½ **cup molasses**
½ **cup nut meats, such as almonds**
1 **cup raisins**
1 **teaspoon nutmeg**
1 **teaspoon baking soda**
1½ **cups buttermilk**
Boiling water

Prepare a water bath or bain-marie using a mold or coffee can or ovenproof casserole for the inner dish, a larger casserole for the outer one. Preheat the oven to 275° F if using a glass dish, 300° F if using a metal one.

Cream the margarine or butter, add the sugar, bread crumbs, molasses, nuts, raisins, and nutmeg. Combine well. Add the baking soda to the buttermilk and combine with the bread crumb mixture. Pour the mixture into a mold or coffee can or casserole, filling it no more than half full. Place the mold, can, or casserole in a larger casserole. Fill the larger casserole with boiling water almost to the top or at least level with the pudding in the inner dish.

Steam in the oven for 2 hours, checking occasionally to add more water.

Yield: 6 to 8 servings

Tip: This can be served hot or cold. Hot is better, but it requires more precautions against burning yourself.

When using a makeshift bain-marie, fill the bottom dish with enough cold water to come halfway up the sides of the inner dish.

Chocolate Bread Pudding

Yes, I know this is old-fashioned and common and not at all the smart dessert in vogue now. But there's something about bread pudding—especially chocolate bread pudding. The scientists might discuss its elevation of serotonin as indicative of its tranquilizing powers; I simply call it a comfort dessert.

4 or 5 slices bread, 1/2 inch thick

2 squares (2 ounces) unsweetened chocolate, melted

2 cups buttermilk

1/2 cup sugar

2 eggs

Whipped cream or whipped topping (optional)

Preheat the oven to 350° F. Butter a 2-quart ovenproof dish. Trim the crusts from the bread and cut the bread into quarters.

Melt the chocolate in a microwave for 30-second bursts, stirring after each, or in the top of a double boiler over *very* low heat. Heat the buttermilk and sugar in the microwave for approximately 2 minutes.

Beat the eggs well and add the melted chocolate. Stir well and continue stirring while gradually adding the hot buttermilk mixture to the mixture.

Arrange the bread in the ovenproof dish and pour the hot milk mixture over it, pushing the bread below the liquid's surface.

Bake for about 30 minutes. Serve hot from the oven or warm, topped with whipped cream or whipped topping, if desired.

Yield: 4 servings

Tip: Check after 10 minutes of baking and push any protruding bread cubes down into the mixture.

This can be doubled. It freezes well.

EGG NOG

Instead of the chocolate, use 2 teaspoons vanilla and 1/2 teaspoon ground nutmeg. Add 1/2 teaspoon ground cinnamon and 1/4 teaspoon ground cloves, if desired.

Lemon Sponge Pudding

There are certain flavors for which buttermilk has a marked affinity. Lemon is one of them. This particular dessert couldn't be simpler, but its flavor is compli-cated—thanks to the buttermilk.

Juice and grated zest of 1½ lemons
3 eggs, separated
1 cup sugar
2 tablespoons flour
1 cup buttermilk

Preheat the oven to 300° F. Grease a 10 x 6 x 2-inch baking dish; fill a larger dish with cold water.

Beat the egg yolks until very thick and lemon colored. Combine the sugar and flour and add gradually to the egg yolks. Do the same with the buttermilk, lemon juice, and grated zest. Beat the egg whites until stiff and fold into the mixture. Pour the mixture into a shallow baking dish, set it in the larger one filled with cold water.

Bake for 45 minutes or until the cake rises to the top and is lightly browned. Serve warm, but better chilled.

Yield: 6 servings

Pecan-Molasses Supreme

This dessert has everything: the sweet syrupiness of a pecan pie, the crisp dough-iness of a cobbler, the tangy spiciness of an apple pie. As I said, everything!

1 cup stirred, scooped, and leveled all-purpose flour

⅔ cup sugar

⅓ teaspoon cinnamon

¼ teaspoon ginger

⅛ teaspoon ground cloves

3 tablespoons margarine or butter

½ cup chopped pecans

½ cup buttermilk, heated

¼ cup molasses

1 teaspoon baking soda

Preheat the oven to 350° F. Grease an 8 x 8 x 2-inch baking dish.

Combine the flour, sugar, cinnamon, ginger, and cloves. Cut in the margarine or butter until the mixture is the size of small peas (use a food processor or a pastry knife). Add the pecans. Divide the mixture and put two-thirds into the square pan, pressing down carefully.

Combine the hot buttermilk and molasses in a large bowl. Add the baking soda (stand back and watch the fun!). Mix well and pour over the crumb mixture in the pan. Sprinkle with the remaining third of the crumb mixture.

Bake for 30 to 35 minutes.

Yield: 6 to 8 servings

Tip: Use at least a 2-cup measure to combine the buttermilk and molasses mixture with the baking soda. The next moment will be dramatic as the baking soda foams up.

Serve with Whipped Cheese Topping (page 118), whipped cream, or Orange or Lemon Sauce (page 111).

Whipped Cheese Topping

> ⅓ cup (3-ounce package) cream cheese
>
> 1 tablespoon buttermilk
>
> ½ teaspoon vanilla extract
>
> 3 tablespoons confectioners' sugar

Cream the cream cheese and buttermilk together. Add the vanilla. Blend in the confectioners' sugar. Beat well. If necessary, add a few more drops of buttermilk. The topping should be thick enough to hold its shape when spooned on the cake.

Crème Fraîche

In America we like our desserts à la mode, or with ice cream. In France desserts come à la crème fraîche (pronounced "krem fresh"). This is a topping almost as thick as yogurt, almost as tart as sour cream, but not so rich as heavy whipping cream.

Actually, crème fraîche isn't fresh; it's aged. Nor is it 100 percent cream; it's whole milk. Full-fat milk. Milk from which not one drop of fat has been removed to make butter. Milk straight from the cow, usually a Guernsey or Jersey, breeds famous for the high butterfat content of their milk.

Although as common as vin ordinaire *in France, crème fraîche is not commercially available here—which, until the development of ultrapasteurization, wasn't a problem. One simply made one's own by adding anywhere from a teaspoon to a tablespoon of buttermilk to a cup of heavy cream, heating the mixture slowly to lukewarm (about 105 degrees), and letting it stand at a room temperature of 60 to 85 degrees for several hours until it thickened naturally. Then the flavor would continue to develop over several days. To truly achieve complexity of flavor, crème fraîche must be épaisse—thick and velvety textured, its taste fully matured like the very best of France's wines.*

Today, of course, live cultures aren't present in commercial buttermilk, and aging ultrapasteurized cream only spoils it. However, if you have fil mjölk on hand (see page 28) and access to nonultrapasteurized cream—through a health store perhaps—you've got it made.

The rest of us can make an acceptable substitute by adding buttermilk to (yes, I know, traditionalists won't approve) "light" frozen whipped topping, thawed. Do it ounce for ounce: For example, if you use 8 ounces of topping, add 8 ounces of buttermilk. Voilà, your own version of aged crème fraîche, which is a contradiction if I ever heard one.

The result is neither sweet nor sour: very good and very different. One can eat it with a spoon without gagging, as one would with sweetened whipping cream. Of course, that's one of the advantages of buttermilk: Its natural tartness cuts sweetness.

By the way, did you know most French recipes that call for crème are referring to crème fraîche? And those that call for milk actually mean buttermilk? Obviously, something happens in the translation!

10 | *Pies*

Plain But Special Pie Crust

Sweet Pastry

Savory Pastry

Water Whip Method

Orange Pastry

Pie-Crust Glaze

Simple Buttermilk Pie

Coconut Custard Pie

Buttermilk Pecan Pie

Old-Fashioned Buttermilk Custard Pie

Lemon Pie

Lemon Meringue Pie

Chocolate Meringue Pie

Chocolate Nugget Pie

Peaches-and-Cream Pie

Fresh Peach Pie

Apricot-Pear Pie

Blueberry Pie

Berry Pie

Banana Butterscotch Pie

Black-Bottom Banana Butterscotch Pie

French Apple Pie

Raisin-Apple Pie

Rummy Sweet Potato Pie

In my opinion, the problem with pies is that they are made with crusts. I believe that if you and I never had to worry about making a flaky pie crust "just like Mom's," we'd all make pies more often. What else would account for the proliferation of graham-cracker and cookie-crumb crusts . . . short pastry crusts and crustless pies . . . pie-crust mixes and ready-made pie shells . . . all to avoid making our own pie crusts?

What makes this fat-water-flour product so complicated? It didn't start out that way. It began life as a "coffin" or pastry casing designed to hold meats and vegetables while they cooked. The crust was not meant to be eaten but to serve as a sponge for excess liquids. Today, the crust seems more important than the filling.

In recipe after recipe, we are instructed to use only ice water. We're told not to mix by hand lest our fingers melt the fat. We are told to cut in the shortening with two forks or a pastry cutter. We are advised to use a chilled glass rolling pin. All for one purpose, to attempt to duplicate the old-fashioned pie crust made with a fat that has an extremely high melting point, which spells l-a-r-d. Any lard crust will be better than a shortening or butter crust. So, what to do? First, lower your standards just a bit: Try for a great pie crust, not a perfect one. Second, use a food processor—much simpler, less time consuming, better in every way. Third, add a bit of buttermilk to the pie crust—the milk solids help give it a golden hue, and the lactic acid tenderizes. Finally, if you want to cheat and be sure it's flaky, add $1/8$ teaspoon baking soda to the buttermilk dough.

And take heart at these words from the past. Said a Swedish parson visiting the colonies of the New World in 1758: "House-pie, in country places, is made of apples neither peeled nor freed from their cores, and its crust is not broken if a wagon goes over it."

Now, you and I, we know we can do better than that, right?

Plain but Special Pie Crust

This is about as basic as it gets, but the simple substitution of buttermilk makes it special.

1 cup stirred, scooped, and leveled all-purpose flour
⅓ cup cold butter, margarine, or lard
3 tablespoons cold buttermilk, or more if needed

Mix the flour and butter in a food processor or use a pastry cutter or two forks. When the mixture is uniformly granular, add the cold buttermilk—just enough so that the mixture forms a ball. Cover with plastic wrap and chill for a minimum of 1 hour.

Roll out and place in a 9-inch pie plate. Bake according to the recipe instructions.

Yield: One 9-inch pie-crust shell

Tip: I like to roll my pie crust out between 12 x 12-inch squares of wax paper. Turn over the wax paper–covered crust frequently while rolling to prevent wrinkles.

SWEET PASTRY
Add 1 teaspoon sugar to the flour and butter before cutting together.

SAVORY PASTRY
Replace 2 ounces, by volume, of the all-purpose flour with whole wheat flour.

Water Whip Method

I hate to tell you how many people have confided in me that they've found a perfect method for making pie crust that I must definitely include in my next cookbook. Well, here it is. A never-fail method taught decades ago in home economics schools. I have been using it ever since. However, for sweet pies, I do as my mother did and add a teaspoon of sugar to the dough.

⅓ cup less 1 tablespoon boiling water

⅔ cup shortening

1 tablespoon cold buttermilk

2 cups stirred, scooped, and leveled all-purpose flour

¾ teaspoon salt

Preheat the oven to 450° F (400° F if using a glass pie plate).

Pour the water over the shortening, beat until creamy, and add the buttermilk direct from the refrigerator. Cool. Combine the flour and salt and add to the shortening. Mix with a fork to make a soft dough.

Wrap and chill. Roll out between squares of waxed paper.

Bake for 10 to 12 minutes or until just barely colored.

Yield: Pastry for one 8-inch or 9-inch double-crust pie, or one 9-inch deep-dish pie crust

Tip: To keep the pie crust flat, prick generously before baking. This does not apply to fruit pies. For fruit pies, cover the dough with aluminum foil and bake filled with dried beans, uncooked rice, dried peas, or even gravel.

ORANGE PASTRY

Instead of water, use boiling orange juice to melt the shortening. When the mixture is cool, add 1 tablespoon grated orange zest mixed with 1 tablespoon granulated sugar. Add the flour and salt, and finish the recipe as usual.

PIE-CRUST GLAZE

For years, women have ensured a golden crust by adding a glaze to the pie before baking. Some use melted butter, others diluted egg yolk, others egg white. But the simplest way to get a golden crust is to brush it with well-shaken buttermilk!

Simple Buttermilk Pie

Here's an extremely simple recipe that makes a simply exquisite pie; it's hard to describe as, like buttermilk itself, it is very subtle.

Unbaked pie shell, 9-inch or 8-inch deep-dish

½ cup margarine, melted

1½ cups sugar

2 tablespoons flour

3 eggs, or 6 egg whites plus enough buttermilk to make ¾ cup

½ cup buttermilk

2 tablespoons vanilla extract

Preheat the oven to 350° F (325° F if using a glass pie plate).

Cream the melted margarine, sugar, and flour. Add the eggs, one at a time; if using egg whites and buttermilk, add slowly. Then add the buttermilk and vanilla. When well combined, pour into the unbaked pie shell.

Bake for 45 minutes.

Yield: One 9-inch pie

Tip: This recipe can be doubled; it will yield three 8-inch pies. This does not freeze particularly well.

COCONUT CUSTARD PIE

Add ½ cup coconut with the vanilla.

Buttermilk Pecan Pie

Despite the custardy filling, those clever pecans end up on top as in any traditional pecan pie. If you like a nutty, not-too-sweet pie, you'll like this.

$^{1}/_{2}$ **cup butter, margarine, or Batter Butter (page 25)**

2 cups sugar

5 eggs

2 tablespoons all-purpose flour

1 cup buttermilk

2 tablespoons lemon juice

1 teaspoon vanilla extract

1 cup chopped pecans

Unbaked 10-inch pastry shell

Preheat the oven to 350° F (325° F if using a glass pie plate).

Cream the butter, margarine, or Batter Butter and the sugar; add the eggs one at a time, beating well after each addition. Blend in the flour and beat well. Add the buttermilk, lemon juice, and vanilla. Stir in the pecans. Pour into the pie shell.

Bake for 55 minutes or until set. Cool on a wire rack and store in the refrigerator. Serve plain or with Crème Fraîche (pages 118–119).

Tip: If using an electric mixer, add the flour to the batter slowly with the mixer going. This way you'll avoid the lumps that otherwise might require much beating.

Old-Fashioned Buttermilk Custard Pie

A very refreshing pie that goes down very easy. It's semi-tart without being sour. This is a modern version of the pie you find in old community recipe books.

Unbaked 8-inch pie shell
3 egg yolks
1 tablespoon flour
⅛ teaspoon baking soda
1 cup sugar
1 cup buttermilk
1 teaspoon lemon flavoring
Zest of 1 small lemon, grated (optional)

Preheat the oven to 325° F (300° F if using a glass pie plate). Line an 8-inch pie plate with the pastry.

Beat the egg yolks until lemon colored. Add the flour, baking soda, and sugar, and stir together alternately with the buttermilk. Place in the top of a double boiler and cook until it thickens, stirring constantly. Add the lemon flavoring and the zest, if desired.

Pour the mixture into the pie shell. Bake for about 30 minutes or until the custard is set and the top is slightly brown.

Yield: One 8-inch pie

LEMON PIE

After removing the zest from the lemon, remove the pith (white stuff) and slice the lemon paper thin; you should have about ¼ to ⅓ cup. Add with flavoring.

For lemon meringue pie, add meringue as directed below.

MERINGUE FOR PIE

Increase the oven temperature to 350° F. Let the filled pie cool to warm before adding the meringue. Use the three reserved egg whites and beat until almost stiff. Then make three additions of 1 tablespoon each of granulated sugar, beating after each addition until the mixture is glossy and stands in peaks. Spread the meringue completely over the lukewarm pie. Return to the oven to bake an additional 10 to 12 minutes.

Tip: To keep the meringue from weeping, spread the egg whites entirely around the pie; do so on a warm, rather than cold, pie.

Chocolate Meringue Pie

This is not a delicately flavored thing but a robust, really chocolaty pie. You can make it moreso by adding the larger amount of chocolate.

Unbaked 8-inch pie shell

1³/₄ cups buttermilk

4 egg yolks, beaten

¹/₂ cup sugar

1 teaspoon vanilla extract

2 to 3 ounces grated semisweet chocolate

Meringue for Pie (page 128)

Preheat the oven to 425° F (400° F if using a glass pie plate).

Line the pie plate with the pastry and chill before using. Heat the buttermilk until steaming.

Combine the egg yolks, sugar, vanilla, and chocolate in a bowl. Slowly pour the hot buttermilk into the egg yolk mixture. Stir well. Pour into the pie shell.

Bake for 10 minutes, then decrease the temperature to 350° F and bake an additional 20 to 25 minutes until set. Remove from the oven and let cool slightly.

Yield: One 8-inch pie

CHOCOLATE NUGGET PIE

Instead of using grated chocolate and mixing with the egg yolks, replace with semisweet chocolate bits. Add at the last minute and swirl, not stir, through the custard.

Peaches-and-Cream Pie

Actually, this is a very simple pie in everything but name and flavor. It goes together quickly. So much so, that making the pie crust will take more time than making the pie. You can guess what I do.

Unbaked 9-inch pie shell
8 to 10 canned peach halves, preferably
in water or light syrup
2 eggs, slightly beaten
4 tablespoons flour
1 cup buttermilk
¼ cup honey
½ cup firmly packed brown sugar

Preheat the oven to 450° F (425° F if using a glass pie plate). Line a 9-inch pie plate with the pastry, but do not prick the bottom crust. Place the peach halves, cut side up, in the pie crust.

Beat the eggs until foamy, gradually add 2 tablespoons of the flour, then blend in the buttermilk and honey. (This works beautifully in a blender.) Mix well. Pour over the peaches.

Combine the brown sugar and the remaining flour, and sprinkle over the peaches.

Bake for 12 minutes or until the crust is golden brown, then decrease the temperature to 250° F and bake for an additional 25 to 30 minutes until bubbly.

Yield: One 9-inch pie

Tip: In place of honey, you can substitute ½ cup granulated sugar plus 2 teaspoons buttermilk.

FRESH PEACH PIE
Substitute 4 to 5 fresh sliced peaches for the canned peach halves.

APRICOT-PEAR PIE
Alternate apricot halves and pear halves. Make the filling using sugar and buttermilk instead of honey. Pour over the fruit and sprinkle on the topping.

Blueberry Pie

One of my fondest food memories goes back to our annual summer trip to Range-ley, Maine. Our vacation house had a blueberry field next door. Every day one of us went out and picked blueberries. We had blueberry pancakes, muffins, waffles, cobblers, and pies—especially pies. This was the one my menfolk liked best. I liked it because it makes over a long period of time. You can start in the morning and do one step then and another at lunchtime and another in the afternoon.

¾ **cup sugar**

2½ **tablespoons cornstarch**

¼ **teaspoon salt**

⅔ **cup buttermilk**

3 **cups blueberries, fresh or frozen**

2 **tablespoons butter (optional)**

2 **tablespoons lemon juice**

Prebaked 9-inch pie shell

Whipped topping

Combine the sugar, cornstarch, salt, buttermilk, and 1 cup blueberries in a saucepan. Bring to a boil and cook, stirring constantly, until very thick. Add the butter, if desired, and the lemon juice. Allow the mixture to cool. Add the balance of the blueberries and chill for at least 1 hour.

Fill the bottom of the pie shell with the whipped topping. Cover with the blueberry filling. Chill another 2 hours or more, then garnish with additional whipped topping.

Yield: One 9-inch pie

Tip: If you decide to let the blueberry mixture sit awhile to cool, cover with plastic wrap, pressing the wrap down on the surface to prevent a skin from forming.

This recipe can be doubled. Depending on the berries you use, it freezes quite well.

BERRY PIE

Substitute other berries, such as raspberries, strawberries, blackberries, or cloudberries for blueberries. Works well for cherries too.

Banana Butterscotch Pie

One of the more interesting aspects of cooking with buttermilk is discovering how the taste of it changes from one application to another. At one time it will seem tart and even sour-creamy; at other times butter-rich; at still other times very butterscotchy. Whichever, it is never strong-flavored, always suggestive, as in this pie which does not have the strong flavor of butterscotch.

$3/4$ cup firmly packed light or dark brown sugar

5 tablespoons all-purpose flour

$1/2$ teaspoon salt

2 cups buttermilk

2 egg yolks, slightly beaten

2 tablespoons margarine or butter

2 teaspoons vanilla extract

2 bananas, sliced

Prebaked 9-inch pie shell

Whipped topping or whipped cream

Bring water to a boil in a double boiler; it should not touch the bottom of the upper pan.

Mix the sugar, flour, and salt in the top of a double boiler; stir in the buttermilk slowly. Cook until thickened, stirring constantly. Cover and cook 10 minutes longer, stirring occasionally. Place the beaten egg yolks in a heatproof bowl, then slowly pour half the custard mixture into the egg yolks. Stir vigorously and return the mixture to the double boiler. Cook 1 minute longer, stirring constantly. Remove from the heat, pour into a bowl to cool. Add the margarine and vanilla. Allow to cool completely.

Alternate layers of filling and bananas in the pastry shell, cover with whipped topping.

Yield: One 9-inch pie

Tip: The darker the brown sugar you use, the stronger the flavor of the pie. I prefer light brown, especially granulated.

You can freeze this and serve frozen if you wish.

BLACK-BOTTOM BANANA BUTTERSCOTCH PIE

After the custard has cooked, reserve 1 cup and leave in the double boiler. Add one 6-ounce package semisweet chocolate pieces and return to heat to melt if necessary. Pour this layer into the pastry shell, cover with bananas, and then layer with plain custard.

French Apple Pie

The use of a custard with apples is very French. And it is particularly good when made with slightly tart buttermilk, which emphasizes the apple flavor.

TOPPING

½ cup sugar

5 tablespoons flour

¼ cup butter or margarine, softened

FILLING

1 cup sugar

4 tablespoons flour

1 egg, slightly beaten

1 cup buttermilk

1 teaspoon vanilla extract

¼ teaspoon salt

5 cups pared, cored, and diced apples

Unbaked 9-inch pie shell

Preheat the oven to 350° F (325° F if using a glass pie plate). Combine the ½ cup sugar, 5 tablespoons flour, and butter to make the topping—it should be crumbly.

Mix the 1 cup sugar and 4 tablespoons flour. Add the egg, buttermilk, vanilla, and salt and beat until smooth. Add the apples. Line a 9-inch pie pan with the pastry, and fill with the apple mixture.

Bake for 30 minutes. Add the topping and bake for another 15 minutes.

Tip: One pound of apples yields 3 cups of pared, peeled, and diced or sliced apples.

RAISIN-APPLE PIE

Add ½ cup (or more, if desired) raisins to the apples.

Rummy Sweet Potato Pie

During my judging of Baked Goods at the Pennsylvania Horticultural Society's Harvest Show, we had a last-minute entry. So late was it that the participant forgot he needed to submit a recipe with the pie. As we judges looked on and ummed and ahhed, the young man dashed off the recipe from memory. Needless to say the pie was judged best in the show—and his recipe was equal to his pie. This adaptation is also a blue-ribbon winner.

Two unbaked 9-inch pie shells

3 large sweet potatoes or yams

3 tablespoons butter

2 tablespoons flour

¾ cup buttermilk

3 eggs, separated

¾ cup sugar

½ teaspoon salt

¼ teaspoon nutmeg

¼ cup rum

Preheat the oven to 350° F (325° F if using glass pie plates) and bake the pie shells for 10 minutes. Boil the sweet potatoes in a saucepan until tender. Peel and mash.

Add the butter, flour, and buttermilk to the potatoes. Whip until creamy. Add the egg yolks, one at a time, beating well after each. Then add the sugar, salt, nutmeg, and rum and beat well. Softly beat the egg whites and fold into the mixture. Spoon into the pie shells, mounding it high.

Bake for 30 to 40 minutes or until golden brown. Serve warm.

Yield: Two 9-inch pies

Tip: The gentleman who made this pie didn't include this information in the recipe, but he confided it to the judges surreptitiously: The secret of the pie is to use Barbados rum!

11 | *Cakes*

Basic Vanilla Cake

Vanilla Quick Coffee Cake

White Layer Cake

Coconut White Layer Cake

Buttermilk Pound Cake

Pound and a Pinch Cake

New-Fashioned Pound Cake

Devil's Food Cake

Very, Very Devil's Food Cake

Chocolate-Cookie Sheet Cake

Chocolate-Cookie Cake Roll

Chocolate Mocha Cake

Chocolate Chiffon Cake

White Chocolate Cake

Spice Cake

Coconut Cake

Coco-Nutty Cake

Rum Cake

Rum Sauce

Blackberry Jam Cake

Berry Cake

Strawberry Cake

Orange Date Cake

Orange Sauce

Prune Cake

Applesauce Cake

Swedish Orange Cake

Swedish Nut Cake

Heath Bar Cake

Cookie Cake

Mrs. Kelley's Chocolate Feather Cake

I love cakes. I love making them, tasting them, and licking the bowl when I've finished making them. I especially love frosting, decorating, and eating them. I don't think there's a type of cake I haven't made—nor many flavors. I am constantly searching for new methods, new tastes, new combinations. However, I am equally aware that what with the eggs, butter, and sugar, a let-them-eat-cake diet is the antithesis of healthy eating on a regular basis. Occasionally is another story.

For those who have eliminated cake from their diets for health reasons, I offer the following suggestions:

To begin with—and you'd never suspect this, would you?—I recommend making cakes with buttermilk. It's low to no fat, low in calories, low in cholesterol, yet it will dissolve the sugar and salt and develop the starch and gluten of flour while its emulsifiers, which help bind the cake together, keep it moist.

Sugar gives tenderness to the cake and enables it to brown. I know of no satisfactory substitute for sugar in cake making. However, you can frequently decrease the amount of sugar by 25 percent without dramatically affecting anything but the calorie count.

Another easy change is eliminating egg yolks and using egg whites plus water instead (for each egg, use 2 egg whites plus enough water to make $1/4$ cup total). And if you like egg substitutes, you can use $1/4$ cup egg substitute for each egg specified. If eliminating yolks only, you can use $1/8$ cup egg substitute per yolk. (And if you do get in the habit of substituting egg whites for egg yolks, I'd appreciate any suggestions you may have for using up all those excess egg yolks.)

Fat is necessary to add richness and tenderness to the cake. First it was prunes, and now applesauce is the latest in-vogue substitute for oil, since applesauce contains pectin which helps retain moisture. If you decide to use pureed fruit in place of fat, definitely use buttermilk in place of any other liquid, and if there is no other liquid, then replace the oil with half applesauce, half buttermilk. Instead of butter, margarine, or shortening, you can use an ultra-low-fat product, but you may not be happy with the results. I'd rather eat a delicious cake once in a while than a not-so-good cake frequently. Otherwise, choose Batter Butter (page 25). Depending on the oil you use to make the Batter Butter, you can make a big difference in the cholesterol. As for the cake itself? I think most are better with Batter Butter—moister, tenderer, butterier. A pound cake made with Batter Butter, for example, has a most delicate crumb and true moistness.

A word about flour: I rarely use self-rising flour because I want to make sure my leavening agents are active. If you prefer otherwise, either eliminate any baking powder and salt specified or check the box of flour for special instructions.

Each recipe spells out what kind of flour to use. If it calls for all-purpose flour which in your area means a hard wheat flour (as compared to the South, where flour is generally soft), replace one-quarter of the all-purpose flour with cake flour.

Also, I never sift flour. If using all-purpose flour, I stir it up well with a fork, use my measuring cup as a scoop to remove what I want, and level the top with a knife (never shake flour to even it). If using cake flour, I spoon it into the cup.

Basic Vanilla Cake

It may be basic, but it's destined to become a classic. When I first came up with it, one of the food editors of Chicago's biggest newspaper said, "Best vanilla cake that I've ever had." She featured it on the front page of the weekly food section.

6 tablespoons butter or Batter Butter (page 25), or

    2 tablespoons butter and ¼ cup shortening

1 cup sugar

2 eggs

½ teaspoon baking powder

¼ teaspoon baking soda

1½ cups stirred, spooned, and leveled cake flour

½ cup buttermilk

1½ teaspoons vanilla extract

Bring the eggs and butter (and shortening, if using) to room temperature. Preheat the oven to 350° F. Grease and flour two 8-inch round cake pans.

Cream the butter with the sugar. Add the eggs one at a time, beating well after each addition. Stir together the dry ingredients and add the mixture, alternately, with the buttermilk, beginning and ending with the dry ingredients. Add the vanilla and mix— don't beat—thoroughly. Divide the batter between two pans.

Bake for 20 to 25 minutes or until a cake tester comes out clean. Allow to cool for 10 minutes in the pan, then turn onto a rack. Frost with any icing—buttercream goes particularly well—or serve topped with fresh fruit.

Tip: In the old days, if you didn't have a cake tester, you'd draft a straw from the broom. Don't do it with plastic brooms; you'll have melting problems. A toothpick works fine.

This freezes beautifully.

Vanilla Quick Coffee Cake

Make cake as above, but pour into a greased and floured 11 x 8-inch baking pan. Sprinkle with cinnamon sugar (1 teaspoon ground cinnamon mixed with 2 tablespoons sugar). If you wish, scatter ¼ cup walnuts or pecans on top and dot the top with small pieces of chilled butter, 4 to 6 tablespoons. Bake for 30 to 35 minutes at 350° F.

White Layer Cake

An extra-light cake thanks to the combination of three leavening agents: baking powder, baking soda, and egg whites. Very tender too.

½ **cup butter or margarine**

½ **cup shortening**

2 **cups sugar**

3 **cups stirred, spooned, and leveled cake flour**

½ **teaspoon baking soda**

1 **teaspoon baking powder**

1 **cup buttermilk**

⅛ **teaspoon salt**

5 **egg whites**

1½ **teaspoons vanilla extract**

Bring all the ingredients to room temperature. Preheat the oven to 350° F. Grease and flour three 8-inch or two 9-inch round cake pans.

In the large bowl of a mixer, cream the butter, shortening, and 1¾ cups of the sugar. Stir the flour, baking soda, and baking powder together thoroughly. Add the dry ingredients to the butter mixture alternately with the buttermilk. Beat until well blended and smooth.

Add the salt to the egg whites and beat until almost stiff. Sprinkle the remaining sugar over the egg whites and continue to beat until stiff. Fold the whites gently into the batter. Add the vanilla and blend.

Bake for 25 to 30 minutes or until the layers are lightly browned and a cake tester comes out clean. Let cool in pan for 10 minutes before turning out onto a rack. Frost with any icing.

COCONUT WHITE LAYER CAKE

Increase the salt to ¼ teaspoon, replace vanilla with 1½ teaspoons grated lemon zest, and, before folding the egg whites into the batter, add ¾ cup shredded coconut to the egg mixture.

Buttermilk Pound Cake

One of the earliest and still best cakes ever. Originally, a pound cake literally meant a cake made of a pound of butter, a pound of sugar, a pound of flour, and a pound of eggs. What no one mentions is that the original moisturizing ingredient was not milk but buttermilk, because the acid in the buttermilk serves as the extra leavening agent needed with all that flour.

¾ cup Batter Butter (page 25) or butter

¾ cup shortening

2½ cups granulated sugar

4 eggs

1 cup buttermilk

½ teaspoon baking soda

1 tablespoon lemon extract

3½ cups stirred, scooped, and leveled all-purpose flour

½ teaspoon salt

Bring all the ingredients to room temperature. Preheat the over to 300° F. Grease and flour a tube or Bundt pan or two loaf pans.

In the large bowl of a mixer, cream the butter, shortening, and sugar. Add one egg at a time, beating well after each addition. Add the buttermilk, baking soda, and lemon extract, alternately with the flour and salt in three increments. Beat until fluffy.

Bake for 1 hour 15 minutes for a tube pan, 35 to 50 minutes for loaf pans. Be sure a toothpick or cake tester comes out clean. Remove from the oven, let sit for 10 minutes to cool. Remove from the pan and spoon the glaze over the top and sides of the cake.

GLAZE

> 1½ cups granulated sugar
> Juice and grated zest of 2 large lemons
> Juice of 1 orange

Over low heat, dissolve the sugar in the juices without boiling. Add the zest and cook for one minute.

POUND AND A PINCH CAKE

Instead of lemon extract, use a pinch of mace or nutmeg (this explains the cake's original name). Cool in the pan for 10 minutes before removing and turning out on a rack. Dust with sifted powdered sugar while the cake is still warm but not hot.

NEW-FASHIONED POUND CAKE

For an even lighter version of this cake, eliminate the salt and use 2⅞ cups self-rising cake flour plus ⅔ teaspoon baking soda.

Tip: For ⅞ cup, measure 1 full cup and remove 2 tablespoons.

Devil's Food Cake

Years ago this recipe was always featured on the back of a box of cake flour—it's no longer there. In my opinion it's one of the best devil's food cake recipes ever. The use of buttermilk, baking soda, and chocolate gives a reddish cast to the cake.

3 squares (3 ounces) semisweet chocolate, melted

1¾ teaspoons baking soda

1¾ cups sugar

1 teaspoon salt

⅔ cup shortening or Batter Butter (page 25)

2½ cups stirred, scooped, and leveled cake flour

1⅓ cups buttermilk

1 teaspoon vanilla extract

2 eggs

Bring all the ingredients to room temperature. Preheat the oven to 350° F. Grease and flour two 9-inch cake pans. Melt the chocolate in a microwave or in the top of a double boiler.

Combine the baking soda, sugar, and salt. In the large bowl of a mixer, beat shortening until fluffy and add the dry ingredients, 1 cup of the buttermilk, and vanilla. Beat 2 minutes at medium speed. Add the eggs, chocolate, and the remaining buttermilk and beat another minute.

Bake for 30 to 35 minutes. Let cool in the pan for 10 minutes before turning out on a rack to cool.

Tip: To make with self-rising cake flour, eliminate the salt and decrease the amount of baking soda from 1¾ teaspoons to ⅝ teaspoon.

Very, Very Devil's Food Cake

This is what my friend and tester calls a "very, very" cake! Very dark, very moist, very rich, very chocolaty, very good!

2 cups Batter Butter (page 25) or butter

2 cups sugar

10 egg yolks

2 squares (2 ounces) semisweet chocolate, melted

3 tablespoons cocoa

1½ cups stirred, scooped, and leveled all-purpose flour

½ cup stirred, spooned, and leveled cake flour

1 teaspoon baking powder

½ teaspoon baking soda

⅛ teaspoon salt

1 cup buttermilk

2 teaspoons vanilla extract

¾ cup mini-marshmallows

½ cup chopped pecans

Bring all the ingredients to room temperature. Preheat the oven to 325° F. Grease and flour two 9-inch round cake pans.

In the large bowl of a mixer, cream the Batter Butter or butter and sugar. Add the egg yolks, melted chocolate, and cocoa. Combine the all-purpose flour, cake flour, baking powder, baking soda, and salt. Add alternately with the buttermilk and vanilla, beginning and ending with the dry ingredients, beating smooth after each mixture.

Bake for 50 to 60 minutes or until a cake tester comes out clean. Let it cool in the pan for 10 minutes before turning out on a rack. Frost the cake and dot the icing with marshmallows and pecans, if desired.

Tip: If you wish to put pecans on the sides of the cake, spread the pecans on the palm of your hand and press the pecans into place.

Chocolate-Cookie Sheet Cake

Not your typical chocolate cake. For one thing, it's made with cocoa, which reduces the fat content of the cake—not all bad from a health point of view. Beyond that, it is a denser cake which makes a good base for whipped toppings or under ice cream or with mixed fruit.

2 cups stirred, spooned, and leveled cake flour

2 cups sugar

½ teaspoon salt

1 teaspoon cinnamon

½ cup Batter Butter (page 25) or margarine

1 cup water

4 tablespoons cocoa

2 eggs

1 teaspoon baking soda

½ cup buttermilk

1 teaspoon vanilla extract

Bring all the ingredients to room temperature. Preheat the oven to 350° F. Grease and flour a 15½ x 10½-inch pan or a deeper 9 x 13-inch pan or a shallow cookie sheet.

Stir together the flour, sugar, salt, and cinnamon. Bring the butter, water, and cocoa to a boil in a small saucepan, stirring until the cocoa is incorporated. While hot, pour over the dry mixture. Combine the eggs, baking soda, buttermilk, and vanilla and add to the above mixture.

Bake for 15 minutes for a cookie sheet, 20 minutes for a 15½ x 10½-inch pan, or 40 minutes for a 9 x 13-inch pan. Allow to cool in the pan on a rack.

CHOCOLATE-COOKIE CAKE ROLL

Make as above but line the pan or cookie sheet with waxed paper. When the cake is removed from the oven, cover with a tea towel or paper towels to prevent a crust from forming. As soon as the cake is cool enough to handle, remove the towel(s) and turn it out onto strips of waxed paper that have been dusted with confectioners' sugar. Cover the cake with softened ice cream, frozen yogurt, buttermilk sherbet, or Crème Fraîche (pages 118–119). Starting from the long side, roll up the cake using the wax paper strips underneath to assist you. Wrap in plastic wrap or foil and chill to firm filling. If you freeze it, thaw in the refrigerator before serving.

Chocolate Mocha Cake

If you're into gourmet coffees and cappuccino, you should like this extra-moist cake, for both the chocolate and the coffee flavors come through.

6 large eggs, separated while cold

3 cups stirred, scooped, and leveled all-purpose flour

4 teaspoons cocoa

1 teaspoon baking soda

⅛ teaspoon salt

1½ cups sugar

1 cup salted butter or margarine

1 cup buttermilk

5 tablespoons strong black brewed coffee, not instant

2 teaspoons vanilla extract

Bring all the ingredients to room temperature. Preheat the oven to 375° F. Grease and flour two large 9-inch round cake pans. Separate the eggs and reserve 1 yolk for the icing. Combine the flour, cocoa, baking soda, and salt.

In the large bowl of a mixer, cream the butter, add the sugar, and beat until fluffy. Beat the 5 yolks lightly and add to the butter mixture. Add the dry ingredients, alternating with the buttermilk, starting and ending with the dry ingredients. Stir in the coffee and vanilla. Fold in the egg whites.

Bake for 30 minutes. Let cool in the pan for 10 minutes before turning out on a rack.

Chocolate Chiffon Cake

The amateur baker who invented this type of cake in the late 1920s sold his recipe for $25,000 some twenty years later. The manufacturing company that bought it got a bargain. Sales of their product soared and cake making was revolutionized because the secret of the cake was substituting a liquid shortening for a solid one. Unfortunately for the oil manufacturer, consumers soon discovered that any bland oil might be used.

½ cup vegetable oil

5 egg yolks

¾ cup buttermilk

1 teaspoon grated lemon zest

1 teaspoon vanilla extract

2¼ cups stirred, spooned, and leveled cake flour

1½ cups sugar

2 teaspoons baking powder

½ teaspoon baking soda

1 teaspoon salt

5 to 8 egg whites

½ teaspoon cream of tartar

Bring all the ingredients to room temperature. Preheat the oven to 325° F. Set aside an ungreased 10-inch tube pan.

Using an electric mixer, beat the oil, egg yolks, buttermilk, lemon zest, and vanilla until smooth. With the mixer on its lowest speed, add the flour, sugar, baking powder, baking soda, and salt. Increase the speed and blend well.

In a separate mixing bowl and using clean beaters, beat the egg whites until fluffy. Add the cream of tartar and beat until stiff. Do not underbeat. Fold the egg whites into the batter.

Bake for 1 hour or more, as needed. (Touch the cake in the center of the pan; if an imprint remains, the cake is done.) Let cool in the pan for 10 minutes before turning out on a rack.

White Chocolate Cake

I found out the hard way that white chocolate varies in quality all over the lot—from a subtle vanilla-y chocolate to a waxy flavorless substance. Although this cake is good enough to overcome even the worst of these white chocolates, it also benefits from your using the best, which is (I'm ashamed to say as a citizen of the Chocolate State, Pennsylvania) the imported kind!

4 ounces white chocolate

½ cup boiling water

4 eggs, separated while cold

1 cup butter

2 cups sugar

2½ cups stirred, spooned, and leveled cake flour

½ teaspoon salt

1 teaspoon baking soda

1 cup buttermilk

1 teaspoon vanilla extract

Bring all the ingredients to room temperature. Preheat the oven to 350° F. Grease and flour three bottom-lined 8-inch or two bottom-lined 9-inch round cake pans. Dissolve the chocolate in the boiling water. Cool. Beat the egg whites until stiff.

Cream the butter and sugar until fluffy. Add the egg yolks, one at a time, beating well after each. Add the melted chocolate. Mix well. Stir together the dry ingredients and add it alternately with the buttermilk to the chocolate mixture, beginning and ending with the dry ingredients. Beat until smooth. Add the vanilla and fold in the beaten egg whites.

Bake for 30 to 40 minutes or until a cake tester comes out clean. Let cool in the pan for 10 minutes before turning out on a rack.

Tip: The better the quality of the white chocolate, the easier it is to dissolve in hot water. With any but the best, I soften it in the microwave in 15-second bursts, then add to the water.

Spice Cake

A dark brown cake that is somewhere between a cake and a quick bread. This is the type of cake you'd want to serve with a whipped topping or a sauce.

2 cups packed brown sugar

¾ cup lard

3 eggs

2¼ cup stirred, scooped, and leveled all-purpose flour

¾ cup stirred, spooned, and leveled cake flour

1 teaspoon cinnamon

1 teaspoon ground cloves

1 teaspoon nutmeg

1 teaspoon baking soda

1 cup buttermilk

Bring all the ingredients to room temperature. Preheat the oven to 350° F. Grease and flour two 9-inch round cake pans.

In the large bowl of an electric mixer, cream the sugar and lard and add the eggs. Combine the all-purpose flour, cake flour, cinnamon, ground cloves, nutmeg, and baking soda and add to the sugar mixture alternately with the buttermilk, beginning and ending with the dry ingredients.

Bake for 40 to 45 minutes or until a cake tester comes out clean. Let cool in the pan for 10 minutes before turning out on a rack.

Tip: Do not substitute butter for lard, which has too high a melting point. Nor can you simply substitute oil for lard without reducing the liquid. Batter Butter (page 25), however, works fine.

Coconut Cake

This is the kind of coconut cake one sees featured in magazines: light, fluffy, standing three layers—and what seems a zillion inches—high.

5 eggs, separated while cold

½ cup Batter Butter (page 25), butter, or margarine

½ cup shortening

2 cups sugar

2 cups stirred, spooned, and leveled cake flour

1 teaspoon baking soda

1 cup buttermilk

1 teaspoon vanilla extract

One 7-ounce can flaked coconut

Bring all the ingredients to room temperature. Preheat the oven to 350° F. Grease and flour three 9-inch round cake pans. Beat the egg whites until stiff.

In the large bowl of a mixer, cream the Batter Butter and shortening, add the sugar, and beat until the mixture is fluffy. Add the egg yolks and beat well. Combine the cake flour and baking soda and add to the mixture, alternating with the buttermilk, beginning and ending with the dry ingredients. Stir in the vanilla and coconut. Fold in the beaten egg whites.

Bake for 25 minutes. Let cool in the pan for 10 minutes before turning out on a rack.

COCO-NUTTY CAKE

Add 1 cup chopped walnuts or pecans when you add the vanilla and coconut.

Rum Cake

A medium dark, very moist cake that doesn't need icing but loves a rum sauce. This is one cake that mellows, tasting better the day, or even two days, after.

1 cup butter, margarine, or shortening

2 cups sugar

4 eggs

¹/₂ teaspoon baking soda

¹/₂ teaspoon baking powder

¹/₂ teaspoon salt

3 cups stirred, spooned, and leveled cake flour

1 cup buttermilk

1 teaspoon vanilla extract

2 teaspoons rum extract or 3 teaspoons rum

Rum Sauce (see below)

Bring all the ingredients to room temperature. Grease and flour a 10-inch tube or Bundt pan. Preheat the oven to 350° F.

In the large bowl of a mixer, cream together the butter and sugar. Add the eggs one at a time, beating after each addition. Combine the baking soda, baking powder, salt, and flour. Add the dry ingredients alternately with the buttermilk to the creamed mixture, beginning and ending with the dry ingredients. Add the vanilla and rum.

Bake for 1 hour or until a cake tester comes out clean. Let stand for 20 minutes before removing the cake from the pan. Drizzle with Rum Sauce, most of which will be absorbed.

Tip: If you want, you can let the cake cool and use warm sauce. This cake freezes well.

RUM SAUCE

¹/₄ cup rum

¹/₂ cup butter

¹/₂ cup sugar

¹/₂ teaspoon vanilla extract

Combine the rum, butter, sugar, and vanilla and heat in a saucepan over medium heat until the sugar is melted. Pour over the cake.

Blackberry Jam Cake

This is one of those recipes I've learned not to tamper with. I'd been making it for years but wondered if it might be too old-fashioned. So, I asked my tester for his reaction. He ranked it right up there, a 10! Liked the dark color with the tint of red. Really appreciated the moist texture. And noted it was one good-looking cake! Another case of why fix it if it ain't broke! (I had thought to change the jam, at least, to strawberry or blueberry or something more common. I was wrong.)

½ **cup Batter Butter (page 25) or shortening**

1 **cup packed brown sugar**

3 **eggs**

2 **cups stirred, spooned, and leveled cake flour**

1 **teaspoon baking soda**

1 **teaspoon nutmeg**

1 **teaspoon cinnamon**

¼ **cup buttermilk**

1 **cup blackberry jam or preserves**

1 **teaspoon vanilla extract**

Bring all the ingredients to room temperature. Preheat the oven to 350° F. Grease and flour two 8-inch round cake pans.

In the large bowl of a mixer, cream the butter and sugar until light and fluffy. Add the eggs one at a time, beating well after each. Combine the dry ingredients in three batches, alternating with 3 tablespoons buttermilk. Fold in the jam and vanilla.

Bake for 30 minutes or until a finger imprint in the center of the cake remains. Let cool in the pan for 10 minutes before turning out on a rack.

Tip: You can double the recipe if you have enough cake pans. Or bake in two batches.

BERRY CAKE

Substitute 1 cup berries (drained if canned or frozen) for 1 cup preserves.

STRAWBERRY CAKE

Substitute strawberry preserves or jam and top with light whipped topping for a low-cal approximation of Strawberry Shortcake.

Orange Date Cake

This cake is a little on the sweet side, which means you don't really need any icing. However, an orange sauce is a nice addition.

4 cups stirred, scooped, and leveled all-purpose flour

1½ teaspoons baking soda

⅛ teaspoon salt

1 cup Batter Butter (page 25), butter, margarine, or
    shortening

2 cups granulated sugar

4 eggs

1⅓ cups buttermilk

2 tablespoons grated orange zest

1 large (16 ounces) package dates, chopped

2 cups pecans, chopped

Orange Sauce (page 154)

Bring all the ingredients to room temperature. Preheat the oven to 350° F. Grease and flour a rectangular 11 x 14-inch pan. Dredge dates and pecans in 1 cup of the flour.

Combine the remaining flour, baking soda, and salt. Cream the butter and sugar until light and fluffy. Add the eggs one at a time, beating well after each addition. Add flour mixture alternately with the buttermilk, starting and ending with the dry ingredients. Add the orange rind and floured dates and nuts.

Bake for 45 to 50 minutes or until a cake tester comes out clean. Pour the Orange Sauce over the cake immediately upon removing it from the oven. Let the cake cool in the pan.

Tip: This cake freezes well.

ORANGE SAUCE

> 1½ cups sugar
>
> 1 cup orange juice
>
> 2 tablespoons grated orange zest
>
> Juice of one lemon

Combine sugar, orange juice, orange zest, and lemon juice in a saucepan over low heat until all the sugar is dissolved. Use while sauce is warm.

Prune Cake

A heavy, moist, brown-black cake that tastes rich but not particularly pruny. Good warm or cold. Keeps for days and gets better every day. If you aren't partial to prunes, or if you're in a hurry, use raisins instead.

> 1 cup pitted prunes
>
> 1½ cups sugar
>
> 2 cups stirred, scooped, and leveled flour
>
> 1 teaspoon baking soda
>
> ⅛ teaspoon salt
>
> 1 cup chopped pecans
>
> 1 teaspoon nutmeg
>
> 1 teaspoon cinnamon
>
> 1 teaspoon allspice
>
> 1 cup buttermilk
>
> 1 cup vegetable oil
>
> 3 eggs

Soak the prunes overnight in cold water to cover. In the same water, cook until tender. Chop the prunes finely.

Bring the other ingredients to room temperature. Preheat the oven to 350° F. Grease and flour an 8 x 8-inch square pan.

In the large bowl of a mixer, combine the sugar, flour, baking soda, pecans, nutmeg, cinnamon, and allspice. Mix the buttermilk, oil, and eggs and when blended, combine with the dry ingredients, beating well. Add the prunes and mix well.

Bake for 1 hour.

Tip: If using raisins, plump for 10 minutes in boiling water.

APPLESAUCE CAKE

Substitute applesauce for the prunes—it's a lot easier but won't keep guests wondering what's in it.

Swedish Orange Cake

In Scandinavia, buttermilk is a common ingredient in all types of cooking, especially in desserts. This was one of my mother's recipes and is one of my favorites.

1 cup seedless raisins, chopped fine

Zest of 1 orange, chopped fine

½ cup shortening

1 cup sugar

1 egg

2 cups stirred, spooned, and leveled cake flour

1 teaspoon baking soda

½ teaspoon salt

1 cup buttermilk

TOPPING

½ cup sugar

Juice of 1 medium orange

Juice of ½ lemon

Preheat the oven to 350° F (325° F if using a glass pan). Grease and flour an 8- or 9-inch square pan.

Cream the shortening and sugar and add the egg. Combine the cake flour, baking soda, and salt and add alternately with the buttermilk, beginning and ending with the dry ingredients. Add the raisins and orange peel.

Bake for 35 minutes. While the cake is baking, make the topping: Dissolve the sugar in the orange and lemon juices. When the cake is done, pour the topping immediately over the cake.

Tip: I have an extra-large food processor and I can make this cake in it. In which case, add sugar to the raisins and orange peel before grinding. Change blades, and cream in the shortening. Then follow the balance of the recipe.

SWEDISH NUT CAKE

In place of raisins, use walnuts or cashews. Chop fine but do not grind.

Heath Bar Cake

It's time for a touch of decadence. We've been so health conscious, so calorie-counting, so cholesterol-lowering. Now's the time to say, so what—I'm going to enjoy life now and again!

6 Heath bars or other chocolate-covered toffee candy bars

½ cup sugar

1 cup packed brown sugar

1½ cups stirred, scooped, and leveled all-purpose flour

½ cup stirred, scooped, and leveled cake flour

½ cup butter or margarine

1 egg

1 cup buttermilk

1 teaspoon baking soda

Bring all the ingredients to room temperature. Preheat the oven to 350° F. Grease and flour a 9 x 13-inch pan. Using a mallet or rolling pin, break up the Heath bars into ¼- to ½-inch pieces.

Combine the sugar, brown sugar, all-purpose flour, and cake flour, and cut in the butter as you would for a pie crust. Remove ½ cup of the mixture and set aside. To the balance, add the egg, buttermilk, and baking soda. Combine the reserved ½ cup of mixture with the broken Heath bars. After adding batter to the pan, sprinkle with the Heath bar mixture.

Bake for 30 minutes. Let the cake cool in the pan on a rack.

Tip: I put the candy in a plastic bag for the crushing process—less messy!

COOKIE CAKE

Use crushed cream-filled chocolate cookies instead of candy bars, but add the topping after the cake has baked for 15 minutes.

Mrs. Kelley's Chocolate Feather Cake

When asked to speak about cookbooks to a "good books" group, I refused the honorarium. Instead I asked that members of the group bring in their favorite buttermilk recipes. This is one of them—and let me tell you, I was more than adequately reimbursed for that talk. This cake is truly light and delicious.

2 squares (2 ounces) semisweet chocolate, melted

1½ cups sugar

½ cup Batter Butter (page 25)

2 eggs

1 cup stirred, spooned, and leveled pastry flour

1 cup stirred, scooped, and leveled all-purpose flour

1 cup buttermilk

1 teaspoon vanilla extract

¼ teaspoon salt

1 teaspoon baking soda

1 tablespoon cider vinegar

Preheat the oven to 350° F. Grease two 9-inch round cake pans. Melt the chocolate in the microwave or in the top of a double boiler.

Cream the sugar and butter and add the melted chocolate. Add the eggs and beat well. Add the flours and buttermilk alternately, beginning and ending with the dry ingredients. Add the vanilla and salt. Combine the baking soda and vinegar and add to the mixture.

Bake for 25 to 30 minutes. Let cool in pans for 10 minutes, then cool on racks.

Tip: When I was given this recipe, I was warned—no butter substitutes. I confess: I use Batter Butter, and it works.

12 | *Quick Breads*

Coca-Cola Bread/Cake with Chocolate Coke Icing

Butler's Lemon Bread

Lemon-Nut Bread

Pumpkin Quick Bread

Pumpkin-Nut Bread

Pumpkin-Raisin Bread

Orange Quick Bread

Corn Bread

Finer Corn Bread

Cheddar Corn Bread

Cheddar-Bacon Corn Bread

Cream Corn Bread

Corn Sticks

Pepper Corn Bread

Armenian Breakfast Cake

Banana Breakfast

Barbara's Butterscotch Bread

Peach-Nut Bread

Peach-Cherry-Nut Bread

Raisin Bread

Mrs. O's One-Bowl Quick Bread

Cinnamon Streusel Bread

Apricot-Nut Bread

It is in the area of quick baking that buttermilk comes into its own. Unlike yeast and baking powder, which require time to do their stuff, buttermilk reacts immediately with baking soda to produce carbon dioxide, and the dough begins to rise just as quickly.

Having said that, why do so many of these recipes also include baking powder? Because quick breads are so dense that they require long periods of baking. Baking powder in its double-acting form (it reacts immediately when mixed with wet ingredients and later under the influence of heat) gives the quick bread an extra push upward after it is in the oven. What I like about using buttermilk, baking soda, and baking powder is that results are guaranteed!

A few tips: When making quick breads with buttermilk, be sure to mix the batter until it is *almost* smooth. Be sure to spread the batter into the corners of the shiny metal baking pan. I prefer the old aluminum or new disposable foil pans. Dark, dull pans and glass baking dishes absorb heat more readily and have a tendency to cook the edges of the bread before the center is done. When that happens, cracks appear in the top crust as the center continues to bake and push upward. When using these pans, either follow the manufacturer's directions or reduce the oven temperature by 25 degrees F.

Cool these quick breads 5 to 10 minutes in the pan, then on a wire rack. Cut with a serrated blade, if possible, using a sawing action.

Coca-Cola Bread/Cake with Chocolate Coke Icing

The name "quick bread" is a lot like "buttermilk"—it's misleading. Yes, quick breads go together quickly and can be baked immediately. But there is a difference of opinion as to whether these are truly breads.

The Coca-Cola quick bread is a perfect example. It is not your typical bread since it's moist and crumbly, but neither is it your typical cake, since it's dense and heavy. Bread or cake, Southerners swear by it. One bite will tell you why. Do some calorie cutting by using Batter Butter.

The Chocolate Coke Icing is the topping when you want to make the Coca-Cola quick bread into a cake proper. It is also very good on spice cakes in general, white cakes in particular, and chocolate cakes as well.

1 cup Batter Butter (page 25) or butter

3 tablespoons cocoa (optional)

1 cup Coca-Cola Classic, not diet or decaffeinated

1½ cups stirred, scooped, and leveled all-purpose flour

½ cup stirred, spooned, and leveled cake flour

2 cups sugar

2 eggs, beaten

1 teaspoon baking soda

½ cup buttermilk, shaken

1 teaspoon vanilla extract

1½ cups mini-marshmallows (optional)

Salt

Bring all the ingredients to room temperature. Preheat the oven to 350° F (325° F for glass or dull-metal pans). Grease a 9 x 13-inch pan.

Melt the Batter Butter, cocoa (if using), and Coca-Cola in a medium-size saucepan (cola has a tendency to expand) and bring to a boil.

Combine the all-purpose flour, cake flour, and sugar. Add the butter-cola mixture and mix well. Add the eggs and beat well. Dissolve the baking soda in the buttermilk and add to the mixture. Stir in the vanilla and marshmallows, if desired. Taste and add salt if necessary.

Bake for 45 minutes.

CHOCOLATE COKE ICING

    ½ cup Batter Butter (page 25) or butter
    3 tablespoons cocoa
    6 tablespoons Coca-Cola Classic, not diet or decaffeinated
    One 1-pound box confectioners' sugar
    1 teaspoon vanilla extract
    1 cup chopped pecans
    Salt

Combine the Batter Butter, cocoa, and Coca-Cola in a medium saucepan and bring to a boil. Add the confectioners' sugar, vanilla, pecans, and salt, to taste. Stir until thickened. Pour over the cake, in its pan, while the icing is hot.

Butler's Lemon Bread

A very moist, very lemony quick bread so delicious it can pass as a cake and need not be buttered. A favorite at extra-special brunches and luncheons.

1⅓ cups sugar

2 cups stirred, scooped, and leveled all-purpose flour

½ teaspoon baking soda

½ teaspoon salt

¼ cup nonfat dried milk

Grated zest of 1 large or 2 small lemons

6 tablespoons butter, melted

2 eggs, well beaten

½ cup buttermilk

⅛ cup poppy seeds

⅓ cup lemon juice

Preheat the oven to 350° F (325° F if using a glass pan). Grease an 8½ x 4½-inch loaf pan.

In the large bowl of a mixer, combine 1 cup of the sugar, the flour, baking soda, salt, and nonfat dried milk. Add the lemon zest, butter, eggs, and buttermilk. Beat at low speed until well mixed. Add the poppy seeds. The dough should be thick.

Bake for 45 to 50 minutes or until a toothpick comes out clean. Cool for 5 minutes and then remove from the pan and place on a rack over a dinner plate. Dissolve the remaining ⅓ cup sugar in the lemon juice and spoon the lemon syrup slowly over the warm bread, saturating the crust.

Tip: To ensure that the lemon syrup penetrates the bread, try repeatedly piercing the loaf with a long, thin skewer. Turn the loaf to each side and spoon the sweetened juice over the sides too.

This recipe can be doubled. It also freezes well.

LEMON-NUT BREAD
Replace poppy seeds with ½ cup chopped walnuts or pecans.

Pumpkin Quick Bread

This quick bread is so dark, moist—very moist—and spicy, you'd never guess it contains pumpkin. One would think it was a spice cake if it weren't so solid.

2½ **cups stirred, scooped, and leveled all-purpose flour**

2¼ **cups sugar**

1½ **teaspoons baking soda**

1¼ **teaspoons salt**

¾ **teaspoon nutmeg**

¾ **teaspoon cinnamon**

3 **eggs**

One 15-ounce can solid packed pumpkin (about 1⅓ cups)

¾ **cup vegetable oil or Batter Butter (page 25)**

½ **cup buttermilk**

Preheat the oven to 350° F (325° F if using glass or dull-metal pans). Grease two 9 x 5 x 3-inch loaf pans.

Combine the flour, sugar, baking soda, salt, nutmeg, and cinnamon. In a large mixing bowl, beat the eggs, pumpkin, oil, and buttermilk until fluffy. Fold the dry ingredients into the pumpkin mixture and mix well.

Bake for 1 hour. Reduce the temperature to 275° F (250° F if using glass or dull-metal pans) and bake for 1 more hour or until a toothpick comes out clean.

Tip: If using raisins and/or nuts, first divide the flour, reserving ¼ cup to coat the raisins and/or nuts before adding them to the batter.

Pumpkin-Nut Bread

Add ½ cup chopped pecans or walnuts to the batter.

Pumpkin-Raisin Bread

Add ½ cup golden raisins to the batter.

Orange Quick Bread

If you're in the habit of fresh-squeezing your orange juice, here's a delicious way to use up all those leftover orange peels—but you must remember to peel the oranges before squeezing them for juice. The bread freezes well.

Peels of 3 oranges

2 teaspoons baking soda

1 cup water, plus more to cover

2 cups sugar

2 eggs, beaten

3¹/₂ cups stirred, scooped, and leveled all-purpose flour

1 teaspoon baking powder

¹/₈ teaspoon salt

1 cup buttermilk

3 tablespoons butter, melted

1 cup chopped pecans

Put the orange peels into a saucepan, cover with water, and add 1 teaspoon of the baking soda. Bring to a boil over high heat; reduce heat and boil for 15 minutes. Drain and rinse with cold water until cool enough to handle. Dry on paper towels. Cut the peels into matchstick slices and return to the saucepan. Add 1 cup water and 1 cup of the sugar. Cook slowly until forming a syrup about the consistency of maple syrup. Set aside to cool.

Grease and flour a 9 x 5 x 3-inch loaf pan. Preheat the oven to 350° F (325° F if using a glass pan).

Combine the eggs and the remaining 1 cup of the sugar and beat until fluffy. Combine the remaining 1 teaspoon baking soda, flour, baking powder, and salt and add to the egg-sugar mixture alternately with the buttermilk, beginning and ending with the dry ingredients. Add the melted butter and nuts. Add the orange syrup and mix well.

Bake for 1 hour and 15 minutes or until a toothpick comes out clean. Cool in the pan for 30 minutes. Turn out on a rack and cool completely.

Slice thin and serve with butter or cream cheese.

Tip: Chill the orange before peeling. It is easier to peel downward in strips than to try to make a continuous peel. Avoid as much of the bitter white pith as possible.

Corn Bread

In the old days, yellow cornmeal was thought common, while white cornmeal was deemed aristocratic. When it comes to cooking, the two perform the same. Personally, I prefer the look of yellow cornmeal, but to each her own taste. And the taste of this crumbly-textured loaf is extraordinary.

1¾ cups water

½ teaspoon salt

1¾ cups white or yellow cornmeal

1 tablespoon butter or margarine

3 eggs, well beaten

3 cups buttermilk

1½ teaspoons baking soda

⅛ teaspoon summer savory (optional)

Preheat the oven to 375° F (350° F if using a glass pan). Grease a 9-inch square pan.

Boil the water over high heat in a large saucepan. Add the salt and sprinkle the cornmeal over the water, stirring vigorously. Cook until it thickens slightly, about 1 minute. Add the butter and remove from the heat.

In a separate bowl, combine the eggs, buttermilk, baking soda, and savory, if desired. Mix well with a hand mixer or whip. Slowly add to the cornmeal, stirring well with a wooden spoon.

Bake for about 1 hour or until firm. Serve hot with jam or jelly.

Tip: If you'd like a crispy crust on the bottom, melt 2 tablespoons margarine, butter, or bacon drippings and place in the bottom of the pan before adding the batter.

FINER CORN BREAD

Replace ½ cup of the cornmeal with ½ cup all-purpose flour.

CHEDDAR CORN BREAD

To the hot cornmeal, add 2 cups shredded sharp cheddar cheese. Stir until the cheese is melted.

CHEDDAR-BACON CORN BREAD

In addition to 2 cups shredded sharp cheddar, add ½ pound diced and fried bacon to the cornmeal-buttermilk mixture.

Cream Corn Bread

This is an old-fashioned corn bread with an old-fashioned corn-bread texture. It's especially good when cooled, and for the next two to three days it improves in taste. If there's any left after that, it begins to dry out—but don't throw it out! Save it for the best corn-bread stuffing you can imagine. From a health point of view, the use of egg whites and buttermilk balances out the fat in the bacon and whipping cream.

1 cup white or yellow cornmeal

¼ cup all-purpose flour

1½ teaspoons sugar

½ teaspoon baking soda

½ teaspoon salt

¼ teaspoon ground mace (optional)

¼ cup egg whites

1 cup buttermilk

2 to 3 slices bacon, diced and fried, fat reserved

½ cup whipping cream

Preheat the oven to 425° F (400° F if using a glass pan). Pour 1 tablespoon bacon grease into a 8-inch square pan. Place the pan with the bacon grease in the oven to keep warm. Combine the cornmeal, flour, sugar, baking soda, salt, and ground mace (if using). In another bowl, combine the egg whites, buttermilk, and bacon and stir into the dry ingredients. Mix well, but do not beat. Pour the batter into the hot pan. Slowly pour the whipping cream over the top of the batter, but do not stir in.

Bake for 25 minutes or until the bread is firm, brown on top, and shrinks slightly from the top. Serve hot.

Tip: Use a smaller pan if you want a higher cake.

CORN STICKS

Use corn molds, or shape the batter into small cakes and cook on a greased, heated iron griddle for 20 to 25 minutes. Serve uncovered so they don't get soggy.

Pepper Corn Bread

Almost a meal in itself, this corn bread is perfect with ham, a salad, or coleslaw. Very colorful too.

1 cup plain white cornmeal

¾ teaspoon baking soda

½ teaspoon salt

¼ cup vegetable oil

2 eggs, slightly beaten

1 medium onion, grated

1 cup buttermilk

1 small can (8 to 9 ounces) cream-style corn

1 small can (4½ ounces) green chiles, chopped

1 cup grated sharp cheddar cheese

Preheat the oven to 425° F. Generously grease a 10-inch round iron skillet (with oven-proof handle) using shortening or bacon grease. Heat the skillet in the oven while mixing the bread.

Mix the cornmeal, baking soda, and salt in a bowl. Add the oil, eggs, onion, buttermilk, cream corn, and chiles.

Carefully remove the hot skillet from the oven and pour half the batter into it. Cover with half the grated cheese. Add the second layer of batter and sprinkle the remaining cheese on top.

Bake for 25 minutes.

Yield: 6 to 8 servings

Armenian Breakfast Cake

I cannot for the life of me think why this is called an Armenian cake, but that's its name and has been ever since the recipe was passed on to me. It is a more delicate cake than most, with just a hint of eggnog.

2 cups packed brown sugar

2⅛ cups stirred, spooned, and leveled cake flour

½ cup Batter Butter (page 25) or butter

1 cup buttermilk, shaken

1 egg, beaten

1 teaspoon nutmeg

1 teaspoon baking soda

Salt

Bring all the ingredients to room temperature. Preheat the oven to 350° F (325° F if using a glass pan). Grease and flour a large rectangular cake pan.

Blend the brown sugar, cake flour, and Batter Butter as if for a pie crust, or until mealy. Divide the mixture in half. Pat half into the bottom of the pan. Combine the buttermilk, egg, and nutmeg and beat well. Add the baking soda and immediately combine with the remaining crust mixture, blending just enough to eliminate flour streaks. Add salt to taste and add to the pan.

Bake for 25 minutes or until a cake tester comes out clean.

Yield: 12 servings

BANANA BREAKFAST

After patting half of the mixture into the pan, add a layer of sliced ripe bananas.

Barbara's Butterscotch Bread

A bread that's a cross between spice cake and gingerbread. While cooking, it smells just a bit like peanut butter. When cool enough to eat, it tastes gorgeous. It is a rather solid bread (it won't raise much), but it's tremendously moist and subtle in flavor.

2 cups stirred, scooped, and leveled cups all-purpose flour

1 teaspoon baking powder

½ teaspoon baking soda

1 teaspoon salt

1 cup firmly packed light brown sugar

½ cup chopped nuts, such as almonds, pecans, or walnuts

2 tablespoons butter, melted

2 large eggs, beaten

1 cup buttermilk

Preheat the oven to 350° F (325° F for glass or metal pans). Grease a 9-inch loaf pan.

Combine the flour, baking powder, baking soda, salt, and brown sugar. Add the nuts, and mix thoroughly. Add the melted butter, eggs, and buttermilk, and mix only enough to moisten.

Bake for 45 to 55 minutes until the top is brown and the edges pull away from the pan. Place the pan on a rack until cool enough to remove the bread.

Tip: Do not overmix or beat; at the same time make sure there are no flour streaks.

Serve warm, serve cool, serve cold—tasters loved it any way.

Peach-Nut Bread

Although technically a bread, it more closely resembles a pound cake in crumb and lightness. Regardless, as my young son used to say, it's dee-lish-us! Butter up, warm or cold, for a snack. Try it as the base for Peach Shortcake or à la mode with vanilla ice cream and more sliced peaches.

⅔ **cup sugar**

⅓ **cup Batter Butter (page 25) or shortening**

2 eggs

¼ **cup buttermilk**

1 cup drained and mashed canned cling peaches

1 tablespoon grated orange zest or orange juice

2 cups stirred, scooped, and leveled all-purpose flour

1 teaspoon baking powder

½ **teaspoon baking soda**

½ **teaspoon salt**

1 cup (approximate) fresh cling peaches, very coarsely chopped

½ **cup chopped pecans or almonds**

Preheat the oven to 350° F (325° F if using glass or dull metal pans). Grease a 9-inch loaf pan.

Cream the sugar and shortening and add the eggs, one at a time, beating well. Stir in the buttermilk, mashed peaches, and orange zest or juice. Add 1¾ cups of the flour, the baking powder, baking soda, and salt to the mixture. Mix thoroughly but do not beat. The batter will be thick. Mix the chopped peaches and nuts with the remaining ¼ cup flour and fold into the batter.

Bake for 50 to 60 minutes or until the bread rises and a cake tester comes out clean. Cool in the pan on a rack for 15 minutes, then turn out onto the rack to cool.

Tip: Use a 29-ounce can of peaches. Drain and mash 2 cups of peaches; chop the balance. If using a blender to mash the peaches, be careful not to puree or liquify the fruit.

PEACH-CHERRY-NUT BREAD

Use a 16-ounce can of peaches; drain and mash the fruit. Add 1 cup (8-ounce jar, drained) maraschino cherries, very coarsely chopped, instead of additional peaches, mixing at the last minute with the ¼ cup reserved flour. Just barely fold in the cherries or the batter will be pink.

Raisin Bread

Why a recipe for three loaves of bread? This makes the best toast! Enough said!

6¼ cups stirred, scooped, and leveled all-purpose flour

2½ teaspoons salt

3⅔ teaspoons baking powder

1⅓ teaspoons baking soda

2¼ cups sugar

2¼ cups raisins

2 eggs, well beaten

2¾ cups buttermilk

7 tablespoons margarine or butter, melted

Preheat the oven to 325° F (300° F if using glass pans). Grease and flour three 9-inch loaf pans.

Combine the flour, salt, baking powder, baking soda, and sugar and add the raisins. To the eggs, add the buttermilk and melted margarine or butter. Combine the wet and dry ingredients gently.

Bake for 1 hour and 30 minutes or until a toothpick comes out clean. Let cool in pans for 15 to 20 minutes.

Yield: 3 loaves

Tip: These loaves freeze beautifully, but thaw before using.

Mrs. O's One-Bowl Quick Bread

This bread just cries out to be part of your repertoire. Provided you have an electric mixer, nothing could be easier. And your imagination is the only limit to the number of variations.

2 cups stirred, scooped, and leveled all-purpose flour

1 cup sugar

2 teaspoons baking powder

½ teaspoon baking soda

½ teaspoon salt

1 cup buttermilk

⅓ cup Batter Butter (page 25) or oil

2 teaspoons vanilla extract

2 eggs, well beaten

Preheat the oven to 350° F (325° F if using a glass pan). Grease and flour a 9-inch loaf pan.

Combine all the ingredients in a large mixing bowl. Beat until well combined. Bake for 45 to 55 minutes.

CINNAMON STREUSEL BREAD

Mix 2 tablespoons sugar, 1 teaspoon cinnamon, and 2 tablespoons softened butter and sprinkle over the batter before baking.

APRICOT-NUT BREAD

Soak ½ cup dried apricots for 30 minutes in orange juice to cover. Drain, reserving the juice, and chop the apricots in a food processor. Fold into the finished batter. Use ⅛ cup reserved orange juice in place of vanilla. Add 1 cup sliced almonds, if desired.

13 | Pancakes, Doughnuts, Waffles, and . . .

Buttermilk Baking Mix

Traditional Baking Mix Pancakes

Apple Baking Mix Pancakes

Blueberry Baking Mix Pancakes

Cornmeal Baking Mix Pancakes

Traditional Baking Mix Waffles

Al Edwards's Dinner Plate Pancakes

Edna Edwards's Baked Pancakes

Joan's Bread-and-Milk Griddle Cakes

Buttermilk Stack Pancakes

Fruited Pancakes

Pinchy-Butter Pancakes

Buttermilk Waffles

Fluffy Waffles

Pecan Waffles

Fruited Waffles

Very Berry Batter Butter

Strawberry Butter

Buttermilk "Honey"

Potato Doughnuts

Lemon-Flavored Doughnuts

Chocolate Doughnuts

Chocolate Chip Doughnut Bonbons

Coconut Doughnut Bonbons

Clam Fritters

Shrimp or Whitefish Fritters

Chicken Fritters

Anna's Fritter Sandwiches

Buttermilk Spoon Bread

Bacon Spoon Bread

Garlic-Bacon Spoon Bread

One of the all-time favorite buttermilk foods continues to be buttermilk pancakes. And for good reason.

Once upon a time, a very wise man conducted an experiment with pancake batters. In one bowl, he put flour and salt and butter and one beaten egg yolk, added fresh double-acting baking powder and sweet whole milk, then folded in the egg white. In the other bowl, he put exactly the same ingredients except instead of baking powder he used old-fashioned baking soda, then added buttermilk instead of sweet whole milk, and again he folded in the egg white. The first batter was thin but thickened a bit over time. The second batter began to bubble and thicken immediately.

When the pancakes were made, he withheld one each from both batters. He noted the buttermilk pancake rose at least half as high again and had a fluffier texture than its counterpart. Forking into the buttermilk pancake showed it to be lighter and more tender.

And, in the final test, the two pancakes were served to a notorious disliker of buttermilk. Although he could see a difference, he couldn't taste any.

The moral? Buttermilk makes it better! And with a tribe of children clamoring for breakfast, buttermilk also makes it faster.

Buttermilk Baking Mix

You can use this for coatings, pancakes, waffles, almost anything—just save the side panels from store bought mixes for ideas. This makes a large quantity. You can substitute Batter Butter for shortening if you plan to use the mix within the next two weeks and freeze the rest. Otherwise, use a solid vegetable shortening.

7½ **cups stirred, scooped, and leveled all-purpose flour**

2½ **cups stirred, spooned, and leveled cake flour**

2 **teaspoons baking soda**

2 **cups dried cultured buttermilk blend powder**

2 **cups solid shortening (do not use butter or Batter Butter)**

3½ **teaspoons salt (optional)**

In a large mixing bowl, combine the all-purpose flour, cake flour, baking soda, and buttermilk powder.

Cut in the shortening by hand with a pastry knife. The mixture should have the consistency of cornmeal.

Store in a covered container (at room temperature during cool months; in the refrigerator during warm) for up to six months. Stores in the freezer for one year.

Yield: 12 cups

Tip: I use my food processor to do the blending. If your food processor is not large, divide the dry ingredients into batches and the shortening into just as many, then process.

TRADITIONAL BAKING MIX PANCAKES

To every cup of pancake mix, add 1 egg, ⅔ cup sweet milk or 1 cup buttermilk, and 1 to 2 tablespoons melted or liquid shortening. If your griddle is not seasoned, I suggest you use the larger amount. Makes 8 to 10 4-inch pancakes.

APPLE BAKING MIX PANCAKES

To every cup of pancake mix, also add ¼ finely chopped apple, peeled, cored, and seeded, plus ½ teaspoon cinnamon.

BLUEBERRY BAKING MIX PANCAKES

To every cup of pancake mix, add ½ cup well-drained blueberries (fresh, frozen, or canned).

CORNMEAL BAKING MIX PANCAKES

To every cup of pancake mix, add ¼ cup enriched cornmeal and ¼ cup water.

TRADITIONAL BAKING MIX WAFFLES

Use the same ingredients as above for pancakes, but increase the melted butter or shortening to 3 tablespoons. Makes two 9-inch-square waffles.

Al Edwards's Dinner Plate Pancakes

This, along with fudge, was my father's specialty. We could count on having it anytime the womenfolk came home late and it was near his dinnertime. Unfortunately for Dad, it did not cure our tardiness. If anything, the thought of these pancakes, so light and melting, the size of dinner plates, did on occasion make us dawdle. (You can, of course, make them normal size—they're equally good, but not half so spectacular as the oversized ones.) And for most people, one is a meal.

6 eggs

1½ cups stirred, scooped, and leveled all-purpose flour

3 teaspoons baking soda

¾ teaspoon salt

3 cups buttermilk

6 tablespoons butter, melted

Separate the eggs and beat the whites until stiff but not dry.

Mix the remaining ingredients until smooth. Fold in the egg whites until quarter-size pieces of white float on top.

Pour approximately ½ cup batter onto a hot well-seasoned (or nonstick) griddle, spreading it out to cover the entire surface. When brown on the bottom, use two spatulas to turn. When brown on the other side, remove and brush or dot with butter or margarine and roll crêpe style.

Serve with pancake syrup, blueberry sauce, or the traditional lingonberry (a Swedish berry that tastes like a cross between currant and cranberry) sauce.

Yield: 6 to 8 dinner plate–size pancakes

Tip: I use a half-cup measure to measure out the batter. It's got a long handle, it scoops up the batter well, and it's easy to clean.

Edna Edwards's Baked Pancakes

This was my mother's specialty. She wangled it out of a dear friend, who had sworn an oath of secrecy to the creator of the recipe. How my mother got it, she wouldn't tell. But since she didn't swear me to secrecy, I can share it with you.

3 eggs, separated

3 tablespoons butter or margarine, melted

1 tablespoon sugar

1 cup stirred, scooped, and leveled all-purpose flour

1/2 cup cake flour

1 teaspoon baking soda

1 teaspoon baking powder

1/2 teaspoon salt

1²/₃ cups buttermilk

Preheat the oven to 375° F (Mother's recipe calls for 380° F; 350° F if using a glass pan). Grease a large pie or cake pan.

Beat the egg yolks until thick and lemon yellow. Blend in the melted butter and sugar. Combine the all-purpose flour, cake flour, baking soda, baking powder, and salt and add to the egg yolk mixture alternately with the buttermilk. Fold in stiffly beaten ("not to death," says Mother) egg whites. Pour into the cake pan.

Bake for 25 minutes or until golden brown.

Serve with maple syrup, Very Berry Batter Butter (page 187), or lingonberries.

Yield: 4 generous servings

Tip: If you don't have all-purpose flour, don't substitute cake flour—it doesn't have the gluten necessary to make the cake hold together.

Joan's Bread-and-Milk Griddle Cakes

This is tender and more moist than most griddle cakes and a good way to use leftover bread. And the nice part is you are incorporating whole wheat without having to buy a whole sack of whole wheat flour. You can double or triple this batch.

1 slice whole wheat bread

1 slice enriched white bread

2 cups buttermilk

1 egg

3 tablespoons Batter Butter (page 25), margarine, or butter, melted

¾ cup stirred, scooped, and leveled all-purpose flour

1 teaspoon baking soda

½ teaspoon baking powder

½ teaspoon salt

Soak the bread slices in buttermilk overnight.

Preheat a lightly oiled or seasoned griddle or frypan.

Add the egg and beat until the bread is broken into small pieces. Add the melted Batter Butter. Combine the flour, baking soda, baking powder, and salt and add to the egg mixture. Mix together quickly and only as needed to incorporate the flour.

Bake on a hot griddle until golden brown.

Yield: 12 to 14 small pancakes

Tip: The mixture should be grainy and/or lumpy. Don't overmix.

Buttermilk Stack Pancakes

I never make a single batch of this. I always double or triple it. I cook all, serve what I need, and refrigerate or freeze the rest between double sheets of waxed paper for use later. These are old-fashioned pancakes, with a thick and substantial filling.

1 cup stirred, scooped, and leveled all-purpose flour

1 tablespoon sugar

½ teaspoon salt

½ teaspoon baking soda

1 egg, well beaten

1 cup buttermilk, or more as needed

2 tablespoons Batter Butter (page 25), butter, or margarine,
   melted, or corn oil

Preheat a lightly oiled or seasoned griddle or frypan.

Combine the flour, sugar, salt, and baking soda. Stir together the well-beaten egg and buttermilk. Add to the dry ingredients and blend until smooth. Add the melted Batter Butter and stir. If the pancakes are too doughy, add up to ¼ cup more buttermilk to the batter.

Bake on a hot griddle until golden brown. Serve immediately.

Yield: Twelve to fourteen 3-inch pancakes

Tip: The frypan is hot enough when a drop of water dances across the surface. To determine when a pancake is ready to turn, watch the surface bubbles. When they begin to break, it's time to flip it over.

This batter freezes well.

FRUITED PANCAKES

Before serving, top with 1 cup fresh or thawed frozen blueberries. 1 cup sliced strawberries, 1 cup chopped apple, 1 cup crushed pineapple, or 1 medium mashed banana.

PINCHY-BUTTER PANCAKES

Blend ⅓ to ½ cup creamy peanut butter into the batter. Peanut butter lovers will adore it.

Buttermilk Waffles

My idea of a great Sunday dinner is waffles! I like to make a batch of them and serve with different toppings. Trouble is that they get eaten so fast that unless the cook gets a head start by stacking them in a warm oven on racks, she's apt to end up working as a short-order cook while everyone else eats. However, take heart! This recipe keeps. In fact, the batter is even better the next day.

2 cups stirred, scooped, and leveled all-purpose flour

1 teaspoon baking powder

³/₄ teaspoon baking soda

¹/₂ teaspoon salt

1 tablespoon sugar

3 eggs

1¹/₂ cups buttermilk

¹/₄ cup Batter Butter (page 25), butter, or margarine, melted,
   or cooking oil

Preheat the waffle iron (some older models will take 10 to 15 minutes).

Combine the flour, baking powder, baking soda, salt, and sugar. In a large bowl, beat the eggs until light and lemon colored, incorporating as much air as possible. Add the buttermilk and then the dry ingredients, blending only enough to get rid of any lumps. Add the melted Batter Butter and stir.

Fill the waffle iron not too full, close it, and watch the waffles raise. Do not open until any visible batter has solidified. If the waffle iron has a light to indicate when done, all the better.

Yield: Eight 6-inch round waffles, or six 8-inch-long rectangular waffles

Tip: The easiest way to remove a waffle from the waffle iron is with a fork.

To speed up the cooking process, always close the waffle iron between waffles to let the baker reheat.

FLUFFY WAFFLES

By separating the eggs and whipping the whites until stiff but not dry, you can incorporate even more air into the waffle batter.

PECAN WAFFLES

My personal favorite: Add ½ cup or more pecan pieces to waffles.

FRUITED WAFFLES

Mash a large ripe banana and add to the batter, or reserve any other fruit you might have to go on top—it's not so messy.

Very Berry Batter Butter

It is my personal belief that pancakes, waffles, and pound cake were created for just one purpose: to serve as an excuse to eat this.

One 10-ounce package frozen raspberries in light syrup

1 tablespoon framboise (raspberry liqueur)

½ cup Batter Butter (page 25), softened

Thaw the raspberries, but don't drain. Process in a blender or food processor until smooth. Strain through a fine sieve to remove the seeds.

Heat the puree to a boil in a small saucepan over medium heat, stirring frequently to prevent burning. Cook for 15 to 20 minutes or until the liquid is reduced by two-thirds, to about ⅓ cup. Remove from heat. Cool.

Cream the butter at full speed for about 30 seconds. Add the reduced raspberry puree, a teaspoon at a time, until it's well blended. Add the framboise and stir.

Serve cold or lukewarm.

Yield: About 1 cup

Tip: If you're concerned about the alcohol content of the framboise, add it to the hot raspberry puree; 99 percent of the alcohol will burn off.

Buttermilk "Honey"

Here is a lovely topping for pancakes, waffles, whatever, that again proves the versatility of buttermilk. Not only can buttermilk be used to stretch butter as in Batter Butter (page 25), but it also makes a mean honey substitute. Although not quite so good as the real thing, it comes very close. And in cases of emergency, it can come in handy. This recipe was used in the early history of our nation and saw renewed life during World War II, when honey and butter were hard to come by.

You can use it in any recipe that calls for honey with the exception of candies; those require a different form of sugar that impedes crystallization.

2 cups sugar

2 cups buttermilk

⅛ teaspoon baking soda (optional)

Combine the sugar and buttermilk in a nonaluminum saucepan and simmer for about 45 minutes over low heat, stirring frequently so that it does not turn into a transparent cheese. When done, it should sheet from the spoon like jelly and be the color of very light clover honey. It should taste like honey with a slight buttermilk aftertaste.

If the buttermilk flavor is too strong, add the baking soda, which sweetens it. However, the baking soda will make it frothy for a few minutes and, if the sugar has any impurities, they will come to the surface. You may need to skim it.

Yield: 1 cup

Tip: If you cook it until brown and then wait until it partially cools and beat it to a smooth consistency, it makes an inexpensive "honey" frosting for spice cakes and the like.

Potato Doughnuts

This is a cake-type doughnut, as compared to a yeast doughnut that takes much longer to prepare. Because of the mashed potatoes—which help retain moistness but which you can't taste—more baking powder than normal is used. The result is a light and fine-textured doughnut with a crisp yet tender crust.

3 to 4 cups vegetable oil

1 cup sugar

1 cup mashed potatoes (leftover or instant)

2 eggs, beaten

4 tablespoons butter, melted

4 cups stirred, scooped, and leveled all-purpose flour

3 teaspoons baking powder

1 teaspoon nutmeg or cinnamon

1 teaspoon salt

½ teaspoon baking soda

1 cup buttermilk

1 teaspoon vanilla extract

Granulated sugar, confectioners' sugar, or cinnamon
   sugar

Preheat the vegetable oil to 375° F. Use an electric skillet or deep-fat cooker if possible. A large skillet will work, especially if you have a deep-fat thermometer. If not, test with a cube of bread: It should start to bubble immediately and brown in 60 seconds.

Mix the sugar and mashed potatoes in a large bowl. Add the eggs and melted butter and beat thoroughly. Combine the flour, baking powder, nutmeg, salt, and baking soda. Add the vanilla to the buttermilk. Alternately add the flour mixture and the buttermilk to the potato mixture, beginning and ending with the dry ingredients.

Roll out the dough on a well-floured surface to about a ¼-inch thickness, and cut with a 3-inch doughnut cutter.

Fry in the order they were cut—do not crowd them—in deep fat for 2 to 3 minutes, turning only once. Drain on absorbent paper and sprinkle with sugar.

Yield: About 3 dozen doughnuts

Tip: If you have trouble rolling out the dough, don't add more flour—it will only toughen the doughnuts. Chill the dough instead.

LEMON-FLAVORED DOUGHNUTS

Eliminate the vanilla and add ½ teaspoon lemon extract and ½ teaspoon grated lemon zest to the buttermilk.

Chocolate Doughnuts

Another cake doughnut, but this one is more like a devil's food cake in the round, thanks to the use of spices.

3 to 4 cups vegetable oil

4 tablespoons Batter Butter (page 25) or butter

1¼ cups granulated sugar

2 eggs

2 squares (2 ounces) semisweet chocolate, melted

3 cups stirred, scooped, and leveled all-purpose flour

1 cup stirred, spooned, and leveled cake flour

1 teaspoon baking soda

1 teaspoon salt

1 teaspoon cinnamon

½ teaspoon nutmeg

1 cup buttermilk

1½ teaspoons vanilla extract

1 cup nut meats, such as pecans, finely chopped (optional)

Granulated sugar, confectioners' sugar, or cinnamon sugar

Preheat the vegetable oil to 375° F. Use an electric skillet or deep-fat cooker if possible. A large skillet will work, especially if you have a deep-fat thermometer. If not, test with a cube of bread: It should start to bubble immediately and brown in 60 seconds.

Cream the butter and sugar together and add the eggs, one at a time, beating well after each addition. Add the melted chocolate.

Combine the all-purpose flour, cake flour, baking soda, salt, cinnamon, and nutmeg. Add alternately with the buttermilk to the sugar mixture, beginning and ending with the dry ingredients. Add the vanilla. Stir in the nut meats, if using.

Roll out the dough on a well-floured surface to about a ¼-inch thickness, and cut with a 3-inch doughnut cutter.

Fry in the order they were cut—do not crowd them—in deep fat for 2 to 3 minutes, turning only once. Drain on absorbent paper and sprinkle with sugar.

Yield: About 3 dozen doughnuts

Tip: Do not rush to fry these. Their sitting a short period of time will not affect their rising, but it will allow the dough to form a seal along the cut edges and thus absorb less fat.

Chocolate Chip Doughnut Bonbons

This recipe makes four dozen doughnut balls, and you'll need every one of them if your family is anything like mine. The bonbons are crunchy yet soft, cakelike yet dense. In a word, wonderful.

3 to 4 cups vegetable oil

3 tablespoons shortening or Batter Butter (page 25)

½ cup sugar

2 eggs, well beaten

2¼ cups stirred, scooped, and leveled all-purpose flour

½ teaspoon baking powder

½ teaspoon baking soda

½ teaspoon salt

⅔ cup buttermilk

1 teaspoon vanilla extract

1½ squares grated semisweet chocolate, or more as needed

Granulated sugar, confectioners' sugar, or cinnamon sugar

Preheat the vegetable oil to 375° F. Use an electric skillet or deep-fat cooker if possible. A large skillet will work, especially if you have a deep-fat thermometer. If not, test with a cube of bread: It should start to bubble immediately and brown in 60 seconds.

Cream the shortening and sugar together and add the eggs, one at a time, beating well after each addition.

Combine the flour, baking powder, baking soda, and salt. Add alternately with the buttermilk to the oil-sugar mixture, beginning and ending with the dry ingredients. Add the vanilla. Stir in the grated chocolate.

Drop by teaspoonfuls into the deep fat—do not crowd them. Fry for 2 to 3 minutes, turning only once. Drain on absorbent paper and sprinkle with sugar.

Yield: 4 dozen doughnut balls

Tip: If you can find mini chocolate chips, use ⅓ cup or more instead and save yourself much work. If you can't find the mini chips, use your food processor to prepare the chocolate.

Coconut Doughnut Bonbons
Replace shredded chocolate with ½ cup or more dried coconut.

Clam Fritters

My husband is not fond of seafood, but he tolerates these, which is a great compliment to the buttermilk. Its very slight tang truly complements the clams.

3 to 4 cups cooking oil

2 cups canned clams, drained

2 eggs, beaten

1 cup buttermilk

2 cups stirred, scooped, and leveled all-purpose flour

1 teaspoon baking soda

½ teaspoon salt

Preheat the cooking oil to 350 to 375° F.

Chop the clams in a food processor. Blending well after each addition, add the eggs, buttermilk, flour, baking soda, and salt.

Drop by small teaspoonfuls into the deep fat. Fry for 2 to 3 minutes. Drain on absorbent paper.

Yield: 18 small fritters

Tip: Adjust the thickness of the batter by adding more buttermilk or all-purpose flour. Remember, the batter will thicken upon sitting.

Shrimp or Whitefish Fritters
Substitute shrimp or a flaky, nonfat whitefish such as flounder for the clams.

Chicken Fritters
Use raw, boneless chicken—a good use for leg or wing meat or chicken tenders.

Anna's Fritter Sandwiches

Talk about a perfect luncheon dish—this combination sandwich and fritter has got to be it. The filling is simple yet extraordinary; the presentation looks much more difficult than it is. And it can even be served as finger food!

Margarine or butter as needed, plus 3 tablespoons, melted

12 slices day-old bread

3 to 4 cups cooking oil

12 tablespoons small-curd cottage cheese

6 tablespoons sweetened applesauce

6 tablespoons brown sugar

1¾ cups stirred, scooped, and leveled all-purpose flour

½ teaspoon baking soda

½ teaspoon salt

3 eggs, separated

1⅓ cups buttermilk

Butter the bread slices. (If you want to be extra fancy, cut the crusts off and save them for bread crumbs or bread pudding.) You will need a deep sauté pan or, even better, an electric skillet. Fill with ¾ inch cooking oil and heat to approximately 375° F.

Spread the buttered side of 6 slices of the bread with equal amounts of the cottage cheese, applesauce, and brown sugar—in that order. Top with the additional bread slices, butter side down. Cut the sandwiches into quarters.

Combine the flour, baking soda, and salt and add the egg yolks, buttermilk, and margarine, blending only until mixed. Beat the egg whites until stiff but not dry and fold into the batter.

Dip the sandwiches in batter coating all sides. Fry in hot oil until golden brown, about 2 minutes per side. Try to turn only once to keep the oil from penetrating.

Serve plain or sprinkle with confectioners' or brown sugar. You can also serve maple syrup if you're not afraid of sugar overkill.

Yield: 24 quarter-sandwiches

Tip: You can use Batter Butter (page 25) in this recipe, but if you made it with unsalted butter, increase the salt to ⅔ teaspoon.

Buttermilk Spoon Bread

I confess, I am a lover of spoon bread. It has the taste of a cornmeal muffin, the texture of a custard, and nowhere near the cooking time of a corn pudding.

1 cup white or yellow cornmeal

1½ teaspoons salt

1½ teaspoons baking soda

2 large eggs, well beaten

4 cups buttermilk, at room temperature

1 generous tablespoon Batter Butter (page 25) or butter, melted

Preheat the oven to 350° F (375° F if using a metal pan). Butter a 3-quart glass casserole dish.

Mix the cornmeal with the salt and baking soda. Combine the eggs and buttermilk, then add to the dry ingredients. Mix until smooth, then stir in the melted Batter Butter. The batter should be soupy. Pour into a buttered casserole, which should be two-thirds to three-quarters full.

Bake for 50 minutes or until the bread is brown and puffy. Spooning into side dishes and serve warm.

Yield: 8 servings

Tip: You can make a puffier bread by separating the eggs, then beating the whites until stiff. Add the yolks with the buttermilk. Fold in the whites after the melted butter is added.

BACON SPOON BREAD
Add ½ pound fried diced bacon to the egg mixture.

GARLIC-BACON SPOON BREAD
Add ½ crushed garlic clove and ½ pound fried diced bacon to the egg mixture.

14 | *Muffins*

The Famous Traditional Buttermilk Muffins

Blueberry Muffins

Cheese Muffins

Apple Muffins

Cranberry Muffins

Whole Wheat Muffins

Fresh Peach Muffins

Strawberry-Nut Muffins

Oatmeal Muffins

Blueberry-Oatmeal Muffins

Bran Muffins, Really Big and Branny

Fruited Bran Muffins

Dozens of Muffins

Cornmeal Muffins

Bacon-Cornmeal Muffins (Quick)

Bacon-Cornmeal Muffins (Not So Quick)

Variations on a Theme

Leavened bread dates back to the days of the Pharaohs, when Egyptians discovered that the foam of beer provided a gas-producing fungus known as yeast. For thousands of years after, beer froth or barm continued to be the preferred form of yeast. And for all those centuries, bread making was a slow, but not particularly onerous, labor that tried one's patience, for yeast is a living thing that does not always cooperate.

Then less than two hundred years ago an alternative to yeast was found. In 1835 a chemist mixed an acid with an alkali and produced enough carbon dioxide to cause a thin batter to rise. The acid was buttermilk, the alkali was baking soda, the combination was tasteless, each component neutralizing the others! That same mixture makes possible our present quick breads, pancakes, waffles, doughnuts, and, in particular, muffins.

Muffins were totally unknown and impossible to make until bicarbonate of soda was introduced to buttermilk. Fifteen years later, foolproof results were promised by the invention of "baking powder," a dry product combining baking soda and an acid in the form of mineral salts. Baking powder could be activated by mixture with any liquid, not just buttermilk or sour milk. It was, however, not foolproof. For one thing, it quickly lost its potency, which made life difficult in those days before date stamping.

For another, it had an "off-taste," somewhat metallic, definitely chemical. So, after the newness wore off, housewives returned to that old standby, combination of buttermilk and baking soda. Ah, but some innovative cook decided to add some baking powder, too, with gratifying results.

In the 1880s double-acting baking powder came along. It produced two different chemical reactions: First, it combined with water to create gas bubbles, then in reaction to heat, those bubbles expanded. The result was much more dependable. But still there was a problem with the flavor. It could be bitter and soapy if too much baking powder was used, metallic if too strong, destructive of other flavors, such as molasses and chocolate, if it were either too strong or too much was used. What's more, the color of the batter might be affected. For example, in the presence of excess alkalinity, chocolate turns reddish—a disadvantage turned into an asset for "red velvet" or "red devil" cakes. On the other hand, to my knowledge, the greening of blueberries has yet to be promoted as good. (Write to me if you have found otherwise.)

Faced with these possibilities, homemakers have remained faithful to buttermilk for muffins. Buttermilk's inherent acidity balances the alkalinity of the baking powder. Moreover, in combination with baking soda, it reacts immediately—an absolute advantage for muffins.

The making of muffins is so quick and easy, cooks have a tendency, in their conscientiousness, to ruin them. So relax and take it easy and, for goodness sake, don't overmix, overbeat, or overexert yourself in any way.

Make a well in the middle of the dry ingredients. Combine the liquid ingredients and add all at once, stirring only until the mixture is moistened—a maximum of one minute. The dough should look rough and pebbly—okay, lumpy! Too much beating will result in muffins with tunnels or air pockets inside.

Grease the bottoms of the muffin cups well, the sides lightly. The idea is to give the batter something to grip while rising. Place the batter into the pan with a small measuring cup, filling cups one-half to two-thirds full. (Generally speaking, a ¼-cup measure works splendidly for an average size muffin.) Fill muffin cups in one fell swoop—don't add a little here and subtract a little there to make them even. Instead of conformity, you'll get peaks.

Also, if you don't have enough batter to fill the entire muffin pan, fill any empty muffin cups one-third full of water to prevent burning and discoloration of the pan.

If you want to convert one of your own muffin recipes into a buttermilk one, use ½ teaspoon baking soda to 1 cup liquid for which you substitute buttermilk. Because buttermilk and baking soda have a leavening effect four times greater than plain baking powder, you must cut back the baking powder by four times the amount of baking soda added. For example, a recipe calling for 3 teaspoons of baking powder would be reduced to 1 teaspoon by the addition of ½ teaspoon baking soda.

FRESH PEACH MUFFINS

Add $^1/_2$ teaspoon almond extract to the liquid ingredients. When the dry ingredients are moistened, add 1 cup diced fresh peaches.

STRAWBERRY-NUT MUFFINS

Add $^1/_2$ teaspoon ground cinnamon and $^1/_3$ cup chopped pecans to the dry ingredients. Fold in 1 cup coarsely chopped strawberries.

Oatmeal Muffins

Because of the use of oatmeal, you may want to increase the amount of shortening. And add salt! Oatmeal cooked without salt seems flavorless to me, but maybe not to you.

¼ to ⅓ cup shortening, melted

1 cup quick-cooking oats

½ cup stirred, scooped, and leveled whole wheat flour

½ cup stirred, scooped, and leveled all-purpose flour

½ cup firmly packed brown sugar

1 teaspoon baking powder

½ teaspoon baking soda

½ teaspoon salt (optional)

1 egg

1 cup buttermilk

Preheat the oven to 400° F. Grease the muffin pans, especially the bottoms—you will need enough pans to make 12 muffins. Allow the melted shortening to cool slightly.

Combine the whole wheat flour, all-purpose flour, brown sugar, baking powder, baking soda, and salt, if desired. Beat the egg well and add the buttermilk and melted shortening. Make a well in the middle of the dry ingredients and pour the liquid into it. Stir with a fork—just enough to blend. The batter should look lumpy. Fill the muffin cups two-thirds full.

Bake about 20 minutes. Let stand for a few minutes in the pan, but muffins are best served warm.

Yield: 12 muffins

Tip: You can spray the muffin pans instead of greasing them, but be sure to wipe the excess spray off the tops of the pans with paper towels.

BLUEBERRY-OATMEAL MUFFINS
Once the batter is moistened, fold in 1 cup fresh or frozen (do not thaw) blueberries.

Bran Muffins, Really Big and Branny

If you're into bran muffins either by choice or for health reasons, then you know the average bran muffin is dry and hard to choke down. Not these, even though this has more bran than called for in most bran recipes. In fact, you don't have to be trying to save your life to enjoy these. They're moist and delicately flavored, they mix up quick (in about the time it takes the oven to preheat), and they are nice to have on hand. When you mix up a batch, bake only as many as you want. You can store the rest of the batter in the refrigerator for up to six weeks.

1 cup boiling water

1 cup whole-bran cereal, wheat or oat

½ cup shortening, melted

1½ cups sugar

2 eggs, beaten

2 cups buttermilk

2½ cups stirred, scooped, and leveled all-purpose flour

2 cups bran flakes cereal

2½ teaspoons baking soda

½ teaspoon salt (optional)

Preheat the oven to 400° F. Grease or line large-size muffin pans. Pour boiling water over the whole-bran cereal and let stand.

Cream together the melted shortening and the sugar. Add the eggs and beat well. Add the moistened bran mixture, buttermilk, flour, bran flakes cereal, baking soda, and salt, if desired (depends on the cereal you use, some are salted). Stir until well mixed. Fill the muffin cups two-thirds full.

Bake for 20 minutes or until the tops are medium to dark brown.

Yield: 30 muffins

Tip: You need not bake all at one time. Store the unused portion of the mix in a well-covered jar or crock in the refrigerator—do not fill the jar too full; allow for expansion. Remove quantities as needed, scooping out ¼ cup at a time, but do not stir the mix down—it may separate.

Muffins will keep for several days stored in a plastic bag at room temperature. The recipe can be doubled; however, you will need a large heavy-duty mixer.

FRUITED BRAN MUFFINS

Add ½ to 1 cup raisins, dates, or chopped dried apples to the batter just before filling the muffin cups.

Dozens of Muffins

A lighter, sweeter, not so branny muffin that still enables you to make a large batch (in the big bowl of your mixer) and store in the refrigerator.

5 cups stirred, scooped, and leveled all-purpose flour

2½ teaspoons baking soda

1 teaspoon salt

2½ cups sugar

4 cups buttermilk

2 cups light cooking oil

4 eggs, beaten

2 tablespoons vanilla extract

~~**One 15-ounce box raisin bran flake cereal**~~

Preheat the oven to 350° F. Grease or line large-size muffin pans.

Combine the flour, baking soda, salt, and sugar in the large bowl of an electric mixer. Add the buttermilk, oil, eggs, and vanilla extract, and when well mixed, fold in the cereal. Fill the large muffin cups two-thirds full.

Bake for 25 to 30 minutes.

Yield: 60 muffins

Tip: If you're really trying to avoid cholesterol, replace the 4 beaten large eggs with 8 beaten egg whites.

Cover and refrigerate the unused batter for up to six weeks, using as needed.

Cornmeal Muffins

To tell you the truth, I could go the rest of my life without eating another bran muffin—I've had that many in the testing of these recipes. But as for corn muffins, that's a different story. I keep looking for new recipes that offer new excuses to make more corn muffins. I think these and their variations are the best of the bunch.

1 cup stirred, scooped, and leveled all-purpose flour

1 cup yellow cornmeal

4 tablespoons sugar

1 teaspoon salt

1 teaspoon baking powder

½ teaspoon baking soda

1 egg

1 cup buttermilk

3 tablespoons melted shortening or oil

Preheat the oven to 400° F. Grease the muffin pans, especially the bottoms—you will need enough pans to make 12 muffins. If using melted shortening, allow to cool slightly.

Combine the flour, cornmeal, sugar, salt, baking powder, and baking soda. Beat the egg well and add the buttermilk and melted shortening. Make a well in the middle of the dry ingredients and pour the liquid into it. Stir with a fork until the dry ingredients are moistened. The batter should look lumpy. Fill the muffin cups two-thirds full.

Bake for about 20 minutes. Let stand for a few minutes in the pan, but muffins are best served warm.

Yield: 12 muffins

Tip: Don't worry if you overmix; cornmeal does not contain gluten, so the muffins will still be good.

B<small>ACON</small>-C<small>ORNMEAL</small> M<small>UFFINS</small> (Q<small>UICK</small>)

Chop 4 to 5 strips of raw bacon and sprinkle over the muffins just before putting them in the oven. Bake for only 15 minutes, then crisp the bacon by putting the muffins under the broiler for a few minutes.

B<small>ACON</small>-C<small>ORNMEAL</small> M<small>UFFINS</small> (N<small>OT</small> S<small>O</small> Q<small>UICK</small>)

Dice 4 to 5 strips of raw bacon and sauté them. Reserve the drippings and add enough oil to make 3 tablespoons. Combine the bacon bits with the dry ingredients and replace the melted shortening with the drippings. Bake as per recipe.

Variations on a Theme

Using the recipes above, you can create your own special muffins.

- Substitute cornmeal, bran, or whole wheat flour for half the all-purpose flour.
- Add nuts, dates, blueberries, apples, banana slices, bacon, onions—anything you like—to the batter.
- Substitute maple syrup for one-half the buttermilk to make a dessert-type muffin.
- Fill a muffin cup half full, add a teaspoon of jelly (or chunk of cheese, slice of bacon, chunk of chocolate, or anything large enough to hold its shape while baking), and then finish filling the muffin cup.
- Make a cakelike, fine-textured muffin by using the biscuit method of mixing. The essential difference is that fat is not melted but cut in with the dry ingredients (as in piecrust making). The egg is then lightly beaten and combined with the buttermilk. Add all at once to a hollow made in the center of the dry ingredients. As if making scrambled eggs, push the dry ingredients into the center, rotating the bowl. When you've gone around the bowl once, stir across the width of the bowl to further mix the ingredients. At this point stir as normal, using as few strokes as possible.

15 | *Biscuits*

Original Beaten Biscuits

Nontraditional Beaten Biscuits

Baking Powder Biscuits

Spanish Biscuits

Lemon Biscuits

Herb-and-Onion Biscuits

Cheese Biscuits

Onion Biscuits

Cornmeal Biscuits

Onion Squares

Freezer Biscuits

Fiesta Biscuits

Sausage Biscuits

Freezer Rolls

Tea Biscuits

Neither-Nor Scones

Raisin Scones

The secret of a good, flaky biscuit is similar to that of a good flaky pie crust: a thorough distribution of fat particles within the dough. That way, when the biscuit is baked, the fat melts, leaving spaces between minuscule layers of dough, which results in flakiness.

There are many ways to achieve this fat distribution. The most common is using an emulsifier, such as lipoproteins, casein, phospholipids, and hygroscopic phosphatides—all of which sound absolutely unappetizing until translated into eggs, milk, buttermilk and/or butter, and Batter Butter (page 25).

Even though our ancestors didn't know about emulsifiers, they still wanted flaky biscuits. Unfortunately, they had no chemicals to do the work. The alternative was to do it physically. Classic French cuisine's puff pastry is an example of dough made flaky by physical means—by literally making layers of dough through repetitive foldings and rollings of dough.

Southerners did much the same thing but without the finesse. Their version dates back to the mid–eighteenth century and is known as Maryland biscuits or beaten biscuits. Over time, many the visitor to an inn in the South has awakened to the puzzling, steady thump-thump of a mallet, ax handle, or rolling pin banging away on biscuit dough; the dough is then folded up and beaten again. For everyday use, an hour of beating was deemed essential; when guests were expected, a minimum of two hours was allocated.

After the Civil War, there were few to no volunteers to continue beating biscuit dough, so Evelyn I. Edwards patented a dough-kneading/biscuit-beating machine. That biscuit beater was the forerunner of today's pasta machine.

Since biscuits by their very nature have no eggs in them, the best way to get a flaky biscuit easily is to use one or more of the other three emulsifiers—milk, buttermilk, or butter.

Buttermilk can be substituted for whole milk in your own recipes, but only real buttermilk—made from whole milk, not skim. My suggestion is that you use a dried churned buttermilk. Home economists recommend it; I go a step further and recommend SACO Cultured Buttermilk Blend dried buttermilk.

In the making of rolls, I have to admit dried buttermilk makes it better—and the use of Batter Butter makes it better yet.

Original Beaten Biscuits

½ cup lard (you can use shortening, but it won't be as good)

3 cups stirred, scooped, and leveled flour, preferably
     high durham

½ teaspoon salt

⅔ cup buttermilk, regular or skim

Cut the lard into the combined flour and salt (you can use an electric mixer; a flat whip works best). Add buttermilk and mix until the dough holds together.

Turn the dough onto a lightly floured board and beat it with a rolling pin or potato masher or, best yet, a small baseball bat. Beating progressively across the surface, flatten it out. Then fold it back up into a rectangle and do it again. Continue beating and folding until the dough becomes smooth and velvety.

Preheat the oven to 350° F. Grease two large baking sheets. Roll the dough out ½ inch thick for large biscuits, ⅓ inch thick for small 1-inch diameter ones. Cut and place close together, but not touching, on baking sheets. Pierce the small biscuits twice with a fork, large biscuits three or four times.

Bake for 30 minutes or until the biscuits are barely tan on top. How much they rise will depend on how long you've beaten them.

Yield: 5 dozen small biscuits, or 2½ dozen large biscuits

Nontraditional Beaten Biscuits

Nontraditional only in the sense that you are adding modern technology to the batter in the form of gas-producing baking soda and emulsifying buttermilk.

¹/₂ **cup lard or shortening**

3 cups stirred, scooped, and leveled flour, preferably
   high durham

¹/₂ **teaspoon salt**

¹/₂ **teaspoon baking soda**

2 tablespoons plus 2 teaspoons dried buttermilk

³/₄ **cup water**

Cut the lard in to the combined flour, salt, baking soda, and dried buttermilk. Add the water and mix until the dough holds together. Follow the directions for Original Beaten Biscuits (page 212).

Serve hot from the oven, split and filled with butter and jam or thin slices of ham. Or serve cold with horseradish sauce for the tenderest, sweetest, best oyster cracker you've ever had. Store at room temperature in an airtight container for one month.

Tip: You can get much the same effect as beating by putting the dough through a pasta machine forty or fifty times. Remember, thanks to the baking soda and buttermilk, the dough will work chemically to rise.

Baking Powder Biscuits

Not all cooks so enjoyed eating that minuscule biscuit that they willingly devoted an hour or so a day to its making. Instead, they were quick to see the benefits of baking soda, and later baking powder—benefits that remain with us in the form of refrigerated rolls and baking powder biscuit mixes à la Bisquick or Benning (see Buttermilk Baking Mix, page 180).

The following may be the best recipe for baking powder biscuits in existence—and it's not new. It goes back more than a hundred years. As the commercial says, isn't it time you taste it again—for the first time? (Which might not make sense for that cereal, but it does for this recipe!) It also gives you a choice of three different types of biscuits from one recipe.

4 tablespoons lard, Batter Butter (page 25), or shortening

2 cups stirred, scooped, and leveled all-purpose flour

1 teaspoon double-acting baking powder

$\frac{1}{2}$ teaspoon baking soda

1 cup lukewarm buttermilk, well shaken

1/2 cup of sugar

Preheat the oven to 425° F.

Combine the flour, baking powder, and baking soda. Cut the lard into the dry ingredients with a pastry blender or two knives—or for the truly hip, a food processor equipped with a metal blade. While stirring with a fork (or pulsing), add enough buttermilk to make a *soft* dough (the dough should begin to leave the sides of the bowl and follow a fork or begin to ball). *Stop!*

Now choose which biscuit you want to make:

1. An easy, no-knead, no-roll quickie that bakes up tender but is irregularly shaped and has a definite homemade texture.

2. A compact biscuit that is very tender and has a crisp crust but requires a modicum of handling.

3. A flaky, fluffy biscuit that just looks and bakes better but requires kneading and rolling.

If you choose #1 (a dropped biscuit), the dough is finished and ready to drop by teaspoonfuls on a greased baking sheet.

If you choose #2 (a patted biscuit), such as those made from mixes, the dough is probably too soft, so add more flour until the dough is manageable. Pat the dough out onto a floured surface and roll quickly until ½ inch thick. Cut and transfer to a greased baking sheet.

If you choose #3 (a kneaded biscuit), besides adding more flour, gather the dough into a ball and knead it gently ten to twenty times—with your fingertips, not the heel of your hand, then roll out and cut and bake on an ungreased baking sheet. It produces a baking powder biscuit worth the work!

Bake for 12 to 15 minutes. Serve warm from the oven.

Yield: Fourteen to sixteen 2-inch biscuits

Tip: Place biscuits 1 inch apart on a baking sheet for crisper biscuits; closer together for softer ones.

SPANISH BISCUITS

To the flour-fat mixture add 1 tablespoon minced green pepper and 1 tablespoon minced pimiento. (If using a food processor, you need only to add chunks.)

LEMON BISCUITS

To the flour-fat mixture, add 1 tablespoon grated lemon zest.

HERB-AND-ONION BISCUITS

To the flour-fat mixture, add 1 teaspoon minced parsley, 1 teaspoon snipped chives, and 1 teaspoon minced scallion tops.

CHEESE BISCUITS

To the flour-fat mixture, add 1 cup grated American, cheddar, or any other gratable cheese.

ONION BISCUITS

To the flour-fat mixture, add ¼ to ½ cup finely chopped sweet onion.

Cornmeal Biscuits

A corn muffin with a cakelike texture. In many ways, these resemble yeast rolls, but they are indeed biscuits! And if your caloric intake allows, do try them dipped in melted butter.

¾ cup stirred, scooped, and leveled all-purpose flour

¼ cup plain white cornmeal

2 teaspoons baking powder

¼ teaspoon salt

¼ teaspoon baking soda

2 tablespoons shortening

½ cup buttermilk

¼ cup butter, Batter Butter (page 25), or margarine, melted
   and cooled slightly

Preheat the oven to 450° F.

Combine the flour, cornmeal, baking powder, salt, and baking soda. Cut in the shortening with a pastry blender. Stir in the buttermilk with a fork until the dough clings together. Turn out on a lightly floured board; knead gently a few times. Roll the dough to about ¼-inch thickness and cut with a biscuit cutter. Dip the biscuits in melted butter and place buttered side up on an ungreased baking sheet.

Bake for 12 to 15 minutes until nicely browned.

Yield: 12 to 15 small biscuits

Tip: Use a metal biscuit cutter if you have one. Substituting an inverted glass, which is sometimes recommended, results in sealing the sides and keeping the biscuit from rising as high as it might.

Onion Squares

Call them what you will—a quick bread, a biscuit variation, an onion pie of sorts; whatever, the result is lovely and a marvelous accompaniment to beef, ham, or chicken.

2 cups sliced yellow onion, or more as needed

2 tablespoons butter

$\frac{1}{4}$ teaspoon pepper

2 cups stirred, scooped, and leveled all-purpose flour

1 tablespoon baking powder

$\frac{1}{2}$ teaspoon baking soda

1 teaspoon salt

$\frac{1}{3}$ cup shortening or margarine

$1\frac{1}{2}$ cups buttermilk

$1\frac{1}{2}$ tablespoons cornstarch

1 egg, well beaten

Preheat the oven to 450° F. Grease a 7 x 10-inch or 8-inch-square pan. In a skillet, brown the onions in the butter until lightly colored.

Mix the pepper, flour, baking powder, baking soda, and salt with a fork. Cut in the shortening (this works beautifully in a food processor using several pulses) until the mixture resembles coarse bread crumbs. Add $\frac{3}{4}$ cup of the buttermilk and mix until the dough is soft.

Spread dough in the pan. Top the dough with the onions. Moisten the cornstarch with the remaining $\frac{3}{4}$ cup buttermilk, then add the egg, and pour over the onions.

Bake for 20 minutes. The top should be glossy with the onions well browned. Serve warm or cold.

Yield: 12 large servings

Freezer Biscuits

An unusual recipe in that it can easily be made into a dinner roll with the simple addition of a second package of yeast and twice as much sugar. I usually double the recipe and freeze half.

1 envelope (2¼ teaspoons) active dry yeast
2 tablespoons warm water
4 tablespoons sugar
1 cup shortening, margarine, or butter
4½ to 5 cups stirred, spooned, and leveled self-rising flour
2 cups buttermilk

Preheat the oven to 400° F.

Dissolve the yeast in the warm water with a ½ teaspoon of the sugar.

Using two knives, a pastry blender, or a food processor with a metal blade, cut the shortening into the remaining sugar combined with the flour. Add the yeast mixture to the buttermilk and stir into the dry ingredients. Mix well. The dough should be slightly sticky, but you can add more flour to make it workable.

Turn out on a lightly floured board, knead fifteen times gently with your fingertips, and then roll out ½ inch thick. Cut with a biscuit cutter—no inverted glass, please.

Bake for about 10 minutes.

To freeze: Freeze unbaked biscuits on a baking sheet, then store in plastic bags. When ready to use, remove from the freezer, dip in melted butter and place on a cookie sheet. Let rise for about 1½ hours or until double in size.

Yield: 18 to 24 biscuits

Tip: If you don't have self-rising flour, substitute regular flour and add 1 teaspoon salt and 1 teaspoon baking soda.

Fiesta Biscuits

Add ½ cup chopped sun-dried tomatoes and 1 teaspoon chopped basil to the dough with the buttermilk.

Sausage Biscuits

Add 2 pounds of roughly chopped bulk sausage, stir-fried and allowed to cool until it can be handled.

Separate dough into quarters and roll, one at a time, into 8 x 16-inch rectangles. Spread each with one-quarter of the cooled sausage mixture, sprinkle lightly with salt, and roll up jelly-roll fashion.

These may be frozen in rolls or cut into ¼-inch slices and frozen on greased baking sheets. As soon as the rolls are frozen solid, remove them from the sheets and place in a plastic bag for storage. Before using, let rise until double in size, about 2 hours or more. Bake in a preheated 350° F oven for 15 minutes or until lightly browned.

Freezer Rolls

Double the amount of yeast and sugar. After kneading lightly, you can shape into various shapes or cut with a biscuit cutter. Don't fold. Freeze and use as needed.

Tea Biscuits

These are not your typical English tea biscuits; those are dry, crackerlike breads. This is the opposite: moist and cakelike. On the other hand, they are not made like your normal biscuit, but like a muffin. In any event, they're very special.

¾ **cup sugar**

½ **cup butter or Batter Butter (page 25)**

1 **egg, beaten**

½ **teaspoon salt**

¼ **teaspoon cinnamon**

½ **teaspoon baking soda**

2 **cups stirred, scooped, and leveled all-purpose flour**

1 **cup buttermilk**

¾ **cup raisins**

TOPPING

½ **cup packed light brown sugar**

1 **teaspoon cinnamon**

¼ **cup chopped pecans or walnuts**

Preheat the oven to 350° F. Grease muffin pans lightly on the sides, heavily on the bottom. You will need enough muffin pans to make 12 muffins.

Cream the sugar and butter. Add the beaten egg and blend well. Combine the cinnamon, baking soda, and 1¾ cups of the flour. Add to the creamed mixture alternately with the buttermilk, beginning and ending with the dry ingredients. Mix the raisins with the remaining ¼ cup flour and stir into the batter. Spoon the batter into the muffin cups.

To make the topping, combine the brown sugar, cinnamon, and chopped pecans and sprinkle over the muffins.

Bake for 20 minutes.

Yield: One dozen biscuits

Tip: If not using batter immediately, cover it tightly and keep in the refrigerator. It will keep for 3 to 4 weeks.

Neither-Nor Scones

Like the Tea Biscuits, these are a hybrid—neither muffin nor biscuit nor roll. The ingredients are those of a muffin, the method of making that of a biscuit, and the cooking that of a pancake.

2 cups stirred, scooped, and leveled all-purpose flour

2 teaspoons baking powder

¼ teaspoon baking soda

1 tablespoon sugar

½ teaspoon salt

¼ cup lard or shortening

2 eggs

⅓ cup buttermilk

Heat an ungreased griddle or skillet to medium. If using an electric skillet or griddle iron, preheat to 325° F.

Combine the flour, baking powder, baking soda, sugar, and salt. Cut in the lard until the mixture resembles coarse meal or crumbs. Add the eggs to the buttermilk and beat until well combined. Make a well in the center of the dry ingredients and add the liquid to it. With a fork in one hand and rotating the bowl with the other, work the dry ingredients from the edges into the center. Moisten all the ingredients, but don't overmix.

Turn out onto a floured board and knead lightly with your fingertips half a dozen times. Gently roll to ½ inch thick. Cut with 2-inch biscuit cutter.

Bake on a griddle for about 10 minutes each side. The idea is to bake the scones from the outside slowly so as to thoroughly cook the interior.

Split crosswise and serve hot for breakfast, or cold in a variation of strawberry shortcake.

Yield: 18 scones

Tip: Like English muffins, these should be split, not sliced open. Once completely cool, they can be toasted.

RAISIN SCONES

Reserve ¼ cup flour and use to coat ½ cup raisins. Fold the raisins into the batter with the liquid ingredients.

16 | *Rolls*

Banana Bonanza Buns

Sticky Banana Bonanza Buns

Sticky Pecan Buns

Sticky Raisiny Buns

Pull-Apart Buns

Herb Pull-Aparts

Whirligig Rolls

Garlickers

Almond Pinwheels

Raisin Rolls

Bacon Rolls

Caraway Rye Dinner Rolls

Dark Rye Rolls

Dilly of a Rye Roll

Refrigerator Dinner Rolls

Salted Rolls

Crescent Rolls

Crescent Cheese Rolls

Plain Rolled Dinner Rolls

Parkerhouse or Pocketbook Rolls

Sweet rolls, dinner rolls, almost all rolls owe their toothfulness to yeast, a microscopic, unicellular plant that multiplies frantically at the right temperature and with the right amount of moisture. Only salt keeps yeast in check—that and limiting the amount of available sugar which yeast feeds on. It is the sugar that is converted into carbon dioxide—the same gas caused by the interaction of baking soda and buttermilk.

Whereas baking soda and buttermilk are sprinters, charging forward at enormous speed for a short period of time, yeast is more like a long-distance runner, covering less ground in a specified period of time, but proceeding onward much longer.

Think of the leavening of rolls as a relay race, with buttermilk and acid as the lead-off runner. This gives the dough an advantage over just plain yeast rolls. Because of this combination of leavening agents, most rolls do not need double-rising as most breads do.

Banana Bonanza Buns

A very moist, very versatile sweet roll with an elusive flavor.

1 envelope (2¼ teaspoons) active dry yeast
¼ cup lukewarm water
⅓ cup sugar
3 tablespoons margarine or shortening
1½ teaspoon salt
1 cup lukewarm buttermilk, well shaken
1 large (¾ cup) mashed ripe banana
½ teaspoon baking soda
1 egg, unbeaten
4 to 4½ cups stirred, scooped, and leveled all-purpose flour
2 tablespoons melted butter (optional)
2 tablespoons brown sugar

GLAZE

1 cup confectioners' sugar
2 tablespoons buttermilk
1 teaspoon vanilla extract
Nutmeg (optional)

Soften the yeast in the water with ¼ teaspoon of the sugar. Let stand until it bubbles. Grease a large baking sheet and a 2-quart bowl. Turn the oven on to its lowest setting for 1 minute and no more. *Do not open the door.*

Cream the sugar, margarine, and salt, then add the softened yeast, buttermilk, banana, baking soda, and egg in a large bowl. Using an electric mixer on low speed, slowly add the flour to form a soft dough. (Depending on the power of your mixer, you may need to work in the last cup by hand.)

Cover the dough with foil or a towel. Let the dough rest for 5 minutes. Transfer to the bowl—rotate the dough so as to coat it with grease—cover, and let rise in the oven until doubled in bulk, about 1 hour.

Roll out the dough on a floured surface into a 10 x 18-inch rectangle. Brush the surface with the melted butter, if desired, and sprinkle lightly with the brown sugar. Roll jelly-roll fashion, from the long side. Cut the roll into eighteen 1-inch slices. Place, cut side down, on the greased, baking sheet.

Preheat the oven to 400° F.

Bake for 20 minutes or until golden brown. While baking, make the glaze by combining the confectioners' sugar, buttermilk, and vanilla. Remove the hot buns from the baking sheet to a wire rack, placed over waxed paper to catch any drips. Brush or dribble with the buttermilk glaze and sprinkle lightly with the nutmeg, if desired.

Yield: 18 buns

Tip: If you can't make all these buns at one time, store the remaining dough in the warmest spot in the refrigerator (usually the top shelf) while the first batch is baking.

STICKY BANANA BONANZA BUNS

Heavily grease (with shortening or margarine, not butter or oil) the sides and especially the bottom of a rectangular baking pan. Cover the bottom with a ¼-inch layer of dark corn syrup (approximately 1½ cups). Sprinkle with about ¼ cup brown sugar. Cut the rolled dough into ¾-inch slices and place close together in the pan. Let rise until doubled in bulk, about 1 hour. Bake for 20 to 25 minutes. Glaze after baking if you wish. Makes 24 buns.

STICKY PECAN BUNS

Before you roll up the dough, sprinkle a ¼ cup chopped pecan pieces inside over the brown sugar. Prepare the baking pan as for Sticky Banana Bonanza Buns (above). Scatter ¼ to ½ cup pecans over the brown sugar in the bottom of the pan. Glaze after baking if you wish.

STICKY RAISINY BUNS

Prepare dough and baking pan as for Sticky Pecan Buns (above). In addition to or in place of the pecans, add ¼ cup raisins that have been plumped in ¾ cup boiling water and then well drained. Glaze after baking if you wish.

Pull-Apart Buns

These buns taste as if butter-loaded, but they don't linger on the hips the way they'll linger on your lips. Tender and light, they separate into bite-size layers.

2 envelopes (4½ teaspoons) active dry yeast

⅓ cup lukewarm water

½ teaspoon sugar

1 cup margarine or Batter Butter (page 25), melted

⅓ cup sugar

2 teaspoons salt

1¼ cups lukewarm buttermilk, well shaken

½ teaspoon baking soda

4½ to 5 cups stirred, scooped, and leveled all-purpose flour

Soften the yeast in the warm water with the sugar. Let stand until it bubbles. Grease a 2-quart bowl and enough tins to make 18 large muffins. Turn on the oven to the lowest setting for 1 minute and no more. *Do not open the door.*

Combine ½ cup of the melted margarine, the sugar, salt, and buttermilk in a large mixing bowl. Add the baking soda. Beat in the flour in three or more additions. Transfer the dough to the bowl—rotate the dough so as to coat it with grease—cover, and let rise in the oven until doubled in bulk, about 1 hour.

Roll the dough out on a floured surface into a rectangle ¼ inch thick. Brush with the remaining ½ cup melted margarine. Cut into strips 1 inch wide. Stack one strip upon the other, 5 to 6 strips deep. Then cut the stack into 1½-inch pieces. Place each section of the stack into a muffin cup, cut side up.

Let rise covered in a warm oven for about 30 minutes. Remove from the oven. Brush the tops of the rolls with buttermilk to give them a gloss and to keep the sections separate during baking.

Preheat the oven to 400° F. Bake for 15 to 20 minutes. They are best served warm.

Yield: 18 rolls

Tip: If you're planning to serve these warm, don't let them cool off prematurely. Don't remove them from the muffin pan. Simply loosen each roll and turn askew so the roll is no longer fully in contact with the metal.

HERB PULL-APARTS

In addition to brushing strips with melted margarine, you can also sprinkle them with a combination of 2 teaspoons caraway seed, 1 teaspoon leaf sage or ½ teaspoon ground sage, and ½ teaspoon celery seed.

WHIRLIGIG ROLLS

Cut rectangle into 18 equal-size strips. After brushing with the melted margarine, twirl each strip lightly about your finger. Drop casually into muffin cups, cut side up. The less uniform the twirls, the more unusual the finished roll. (Rolls will take different shapes as they rise.)

GARLICKERS

Before brushing on the melted margarine, add garlic juice or crushed garlic. Proceed as for regular Pull-Apart Buns.

Almond Pinwheels

A sweet roll with a very subtle flavor—the combination of molasses, sweet brown sugar, tangy buttermilk, and nutty almond extract. This is an excellent dough to make in a food processor if you have a large one.

1 envelope (2¼ teaspoons) active dry yeast

¼ cup lukewarm water

¼ teaspoon plus 1 tablespoon sugar

¾ cup Batter Butter (page 25) or ½ cup butter shortening

3¼ cups stirred, scooped, and leveled all-purpose flour

2 eggs

⅔ cup lukewarm buttermilk, well shaken

¼ teaspoon baking soda

1 teaspoon almond extract

¾ cup firmly packed brown sugar

½ cup almonds, chopped

Dissolve the yeast in the warm, not hot, water with ¼ teaspoon of the sugar. Let stand until it bubbles.

Process the Batter Butter and flour in a food processor until the size of small peas. With the processor still running, add the eggs, buttermilk, sugar, baking soda, almond extract, and softened yeast—just until the mixture forms a ball. Transfer to a large greased bowl and chill, covered, for 2 hours.

Spread the brown sugar over a lightly floured surface. Roll the dough out in the sugar with a rolling pin, turning, folding, flipping, and rerolling until all the sugar is used. Roll out the dough approximately 20 inches long and ¼ inch thick. Sprinkle the chopped almonds over the dough, pressing them in with a rolling pin.

Roll the dough up jelly-roll fashion and cut into 24 medium-size rolls or 36 small ones. Place on greased baking sheets. Turn on the oven to the lowest setting for 1 minute and no more. Place the baking sheets in the oven and let the rolls rise until light, about 30 minutes. Remove the rolls from the oven.

Preheat the oven to 400° F. Bake for 15 to 20 minutes, depending on size of the rolls.

Yield: 24 to 36 rolls

Tip: Life will be a lot simpler—and so will the making of these rolls—if you use granulated brown sugar.

RAISIN ROLLS

In place of almonds, sprinkle raisins (I prefer the golden ones).

BACON ROLLS

In addition to or in place of brown sugar, use 4 slices lightly cooked and crumbled well-drained bacon pieces. Remember, they will cook more during baking.

Caraway Rye Dinner Rolls

No kneading to this dinner roll, or rolling either. Simply drop into unlined muffin pans, let rise, and bake. My husband loves these with corned beef and cabbage.

1 envelope (2¼ teaspoons) active dry yeast

¼ cup lukewarm water

¼ teaspoon sugar

¼ cup margarine or Batter Butter (page 25)

1 cup lukewarm buttermilk, well shaken

¼ cup molasses

1 teaspoon salt

2 teaspoons caraway seeds

1 egg

1 cup stirred, scooped, and leveled rye flour

1 teaspoon double-acting baking powder

½ teaspoon baking soda

2½ to 3 cups stirred, scooped, and leveled all-purpose flour

Dissolve the yeast in the warm water with the sugar. Let stand until it bubbles. Grease enough muffin pans for 18 to 24 rolls.

Combine the margarine, buttermilk, molasses, salt, and caraway seeds in the large bowl of an electric mixer. Be sure the yeast mixture is lukewarm before adding. Add the egg, and with the mixer running at low speed, add the rye flour, baking powder, and baking soda. Increase the speed to medium and beat well. Beat in the all-purpose flour in three or more additions. When it forms a soft dough, stop the mixer.

Turn on the oven to the lowest setting for 1 minute. Fill muffin cups about one-half full. (If you wish, brush the rolls with buttermilk to make them crusty on top.) Cover and place in the oven to warm until doubled in bulk, about 2 hours. Remove the rolls from the oven.

Preheat the oven to 400° F. Bake for 15 to 20 minutes. Serve warm or cold.

Yield: 18 to 24 rolls

DARK RYE ROLLS

Bakers choose from among a variety of flours to achieve a dark rye. There is an easier way: add $1/8$ cup unsweetened cocoa.

DILLY OF A RYE ROLL

Replace 1 teaspoon of the caraway seeds with 1 teaspoon dill seeds and 1 teaspoon dillweed.

Refrigerator Dinner Rolls

*Although this dough takes longer to make—it requires a complete double ris-
ing—it has the advantage of not needing kneading, and it can be made up to a
week in advance. Store the dough in the refrigerator and bake as needed.*

1 envelope (2¼ teaspoons) active dry yeast

¼ cup lukewarm water

¼ teaspoon sugar

½ cup margarine, shortening, or Batter Butter (page 25)

⅓ cup sugar

1¾ cup lukewarm buttermilk, well shaken, plus more as
    needed for glaze

1 egg

3 cups stirred, scooped, and leveled all-purpose flour, plus
    more as needed for rolling

1½ teaspoons salt

1 teaspoon double-acting baking powder

½ teaspoon baking soda

Dissolve the yeast in the warm water with the sugar. Let stand until it bubbles. Grease
large muffin pans and a 2-quart bowl. Turn on the oven to the lowest setting for
1 minute and no more. *Do not open the door.*

Combine the margarine, sugar, and buttermilk. Add the egg and the softened yeast.
Stir the dry ingredients together and blend into the yeast mixture to form a soft dough.
Transfer to the large bowl, cover, and put in the oven for about 1 hour or until doubled
in bulk.

Remove the dough from the bowl and place on a well-floured surface. Turn and toss
the dough, adding flour as necessary, until the dough is no longer sticky. Shape now or
refrigerate until needed.

At least 3 hours before using, remove the dough from the refrigerator. To make
cloverleafs, divide the dough into four parts. Make the first part into 18 round balls
about 1 inch in diameter. Place three at a time in the greased muffin cups to form a

cloverleaf. Continue with other portions of the dough if you wish or return them to the refrigerator. Brush the shaped biscuits with buttermilk to help keep the cloverleafs distinct while rising and baking. Let rise in the warm oven until double in bulk, about 2 to 3 hours.

Preheat the oven to 400° F. Bake for 15 to 20 minutes.

Yield: 24 large cloverleafs

Tip: If you are using previously refrigerated dough, expect the second rising—the one after shaping—to take anywhere from 2 to 3 hours, depending on the temperature of the dough and the room. Also, if the dough rises while refrigerated, simply punch it down and return it to refrigerator.

SALTED ROLLS

To the buttermilk for the glaze, add 1 tablespoon sea or kosher salt.

CRESCENT ROLLS

Instead of taking each portion and shaping it into balls, roll each portion into a circle about 8 inches in diameter. Brush with butter or margarine. Cut into 8 wedges. Starting at the wide end, roll each wedge toward a point. Place on a greased, sprayed, or oiled baking sheet, pointed side down. Let rise as needed and bake for 15 to 18 minutes.

CRESCENT CHEESE ROLLS

Proceed as above for Crescent Rolls, then after brushing with butter, sprinkle with any grated hard cheese (I prefer Parmesan). Be frugal with it; otherwise it will simply melt all over the baking sheet.

Plain Rolled Dinner Rolls

Actually there's nothing plain about these dinner rolls—they're tender, light, and fit for company.

1 envelope (2¼ teaspoons) active dry yeast

2 tablespoons sugar

2 cups lukewarm buttermilk, plus more as needed

3 tablespoons Batter Butter (page 25) or margarine

½ teaspoon baking soda

½ teaspoon baking powder

2 teaspoons salt

4 cups stirred, scooped, and leveled all-purpose flour

2 tablespoons butter, melted

Dissolve the yeast with ¼ teaspoon of the sugar in ½ cup of the warm buttermilk. Grease the baking pans (I use round layer cake pans).

In the large bowl of an electric mixer, cream the remaining sugar and the margarine together and add the softened yeast. Combine the baking soda, baking powder, salt, and flour and add, alternately, with the remaining 1½ cups of the buttermilk, beating thoroughly between each addition. At the end, you may have to work in the flour by hand.

Turn the dough out onto a floured surface and knead until smooth and elastic. Roll the dough out ½ inch thick and cut with a 2-inch biscuit cutter. Place evenly spread apart on the baking pans. Brush with more buttermilk, cover, and let rise in a warm place until light, about 45 minutes to 1 hour.

Preheat the oven to 425° F. Bake for 20 to 25 minutes or until golden brown.

Yield: 18 biscuits

Tip: Dip a cutter into the flour before cutting the dough. If you don't have a cutter, an inverted juice or water glass is *not* a satisfactory substitute; it will crush the dough. Try using a clean tin can with a sharp edge. Or use a glass to make a pattern and cut with a knife.

PARKERHOUSE OR POCKETBOOK ROLLS

When the dough has been rolled out, cut with a 3-inch cutter, brush with melted butter, and crease off-center with a dinner knife. Fold the short half back over the larger half and press to make a modified Parkerhouse or pocketbook roll.

17 | *Breads*

My Absolutely Favorite Basic White Bread

Beer Bread

Half 'n' Half Bread

Whole Wheat Bread

Raisin Bread

P.D.Q. White Bread

P.D.Q. Cheese Bread

P.D.Q. Sweet Bread

P.D.Q. Sweet Cinnamon Bread

Quickie Buttermilk Bread Loaves

White Soda Bread

Raisin or Currant Soda Bread

Walnut-Dill Soda Bread

Lemon–Poppy Seed Soda Bread

British-Irish Soda Bread

Whole Wheat "Honey" Bread

Oh, how I love bread making. The smell of the yeast! Better than fancy, schmantzy perfume. The feel of the dough growing softer and smoother beneath my hands. The kneading: pull, push, fold, turn—more productive than throwing punches at a punching bag. The way it puffs. The moment of anticipation before your fist plows into it, deflating it as you'd love to deflate all the blowhards in the world. But you know as well as I do that that dough won't stay deflated any longer than a sticky-fingered fellow will stay embarrassed after having been caught with his hand in the till.

And the baking! If one has a glass door to the oven, one can watch that bread pushing proudly upward—the gentle, golden browning. Otherwise, one sneaks peaks, opening only a crack so as not to let any drafts into the oven to underdo your work. "In a minute," you say to the innumerable questions of "Is it done yet?"

Then the timer goes off. And teenagers who can sleep through the whir of the vacuum, the sound of the lawn mower, the persistent ring of the alarm clock—those self-same teenagers are suddenly there to watch you take the pan out of the oven and turn it on its side and release the loaf. A rap on the bottom of the pan. Echoed hopefully by a thumping hollow sound that says, "I'm done. I'm done." And then after what seems an unendurable wait, the first slice! Everyone fights for it—even those who never eat their crusts.

So much do I love making bread that everyone chipped in at Christmas to give me a bread machine. I admit, it's easy. Bread chugs along all by itself, noiselessly, odorlessly, unobservedly. It proofs, it mixes, it raises, it bakes, it turns itself off—heck, it does everything but slice itself. The one thing it doesn't do is end up looking like bread—instead it looks like a snub-nosed missile. And who wants bread that's the same round shape as bologna and mozzarella and tomatoes? Takes all the fun out of it.

I admit, you may not feel as I do. Therefore, you may want to compare these recipes for buttermilk breads to recipes supplied with your bread machine. I think you'll find most work swell being made automatically—darn it!

About kneading: Look, Mom, one hand! Place the dough in front of you and sprinkle it with flour; dip your working hand in flour also. Using the heel of that hand, push down and into the dough. Fold in the farthest side toward you and give the dough a quarter turn to your right and push again. Repeat until the dough is smooth and elastic. If you have very small hands or are more comfortable using both, by all means do; I'm not going to tell.

My Absolutely Favorite Basic White Bread

It started life better than thirty years ago as a white bread recipe from Joy of Cooking. *I have made it with water, beer, buttermilk, you name it. And never has it failed me, although it has metamorphosed a bit. Whenever I have excess energy or anger to work off, I make this bread—it takes a lot of kneading.*

2 tablespoons Batter Butter (page 25), melted, or
  1 tablespoon *each* **lard and butter, melted**
2 tablespoons sugar
2½ teaspoons salt
2 cups buttermilk
1 envelope (2¼ teaspoons) active dry yeast
¼ cup warm water
6½ cups stirred, scooped, and leveled all-purpose flour

Combine the melted Batter Butter with the sugar, salt, and buttermilk. Cool to lukewarm and sprinkle with the yeast. Stir in the water. Place the mixture in a large bowl of a mixer and, with the mixer barely moving, stir in 3 cups of the flour. Increase the speed and beat the batter for 1 minute. Decrease the speed, add the remaining 3 cups flour, and beat until well combined.

Toss the dough onto a floured surface and knead it until the dough no longer sticks to the board and is elastic, smooth, and full of bubbles. Place in a greased bowl, rotate to cover all the dough with grease, cover with a towel, and allow to rise in a warm place until doubled in bulk, about 1 hour.

Remove the dough from the bowl and knead it back to its original bulk, then let it rise again for about 1½ hours. Shape into two loaves and place in greased shiny 5 x 10-inch pans, filling each half full. Let the dough rise again until doubled in bulk.

Preheat the oven to 450° F (425° F if using glass or dull-metal pans). Bake for 10 minutes. Reduce the heat to 350° F (325° F if using glass or dull-metal pans) and bake until it shrinks from the side of the pan, about 40 minutes total. Remove from the pans and cool on racks. (I turn the loaves on their sides.)

Yield: 2 loaves

BEER BREAD
Replace the buttermilk with beer—not flat, but not too much foam, please.

HALF 'N' HALF BREAD
Use 1 cup buttermilk and 1 cup water or regular milk, or 1 cup regular milk and 1 cup water.

WHOLE WHEAT BREAD
Replace 3¼ cups of the flour with whole wheat flour.

RAISIN BREAD
Reserve 1 cup flour, sprinkle over seeded raisins, and add with the yeast.

P.D.Q. White Bread

About twenty or twenty-five years ago, home economists working in the kitchens of various flour companies came up with a quick method of making bread. They called it Can Do Quick. Mothers, at least on the East Coast, rechristened it P.D.Q. Essentially it is an extension of the double-leavened roll, in that it has both yeast and baking powder/baking soda to get things moving. This particular one has a nice crumb and a good crust. Not sweet, it has a touch of tang to it.

2 envelopes (4½ teaspoons) active dry yeast

¾ cup warm water

½ teaspoon sugar

1¼ cups lukewarm buttermilk

4½ to 5½ cups stirred, scooped, and leveled all-purpose
   flour

5½ teaspoons sugar

2 teaspoons baking powder

2 teaspoons salt

¼ cup lard, margarine, or shortening, softened

2 tablespoons butter, melted

Dissolve the yeast in warm water with the sugar added. Stirring by hand speeds up the action. Set aside until it dissolves and foams and gives off a distinctive yeasty fragrance—approximately 3 minutes. Put a large pan of boiling water on the bottom rack of a cold oven. Grease one 9 x 5-inch shiny loaf pan.

Add the buttermilk, 2½ cups of the flour, the sugar, baking powder, salt, and lard to the yeast. Mix on low for approximately 30 seconds or until the flour has been completely incorporated. Scrape down the sides, increase the mixer speed to medium, and beat for 2 minutes.

If using a heavy duty mixer, reduce the speed to low and gradually blend in 2 more cups flour; otherwise stir in the flour by hand. The dough should be soft and a bit sticky. If too sticky to handle, add more flour in ¼ cup increments.

If you have a dough hook, knead in a mixer for about 4 minutes, adding small amounts of flour if the dough remains too sticky. Otherwise, turn the dough out on a well-floured surface and knead for 6 minutes or more until the dough is smooth and elastic, adding flour as needed.

If you like a fine textured bread without air holes, roll out the dough with a rolling pin into a rectangle 10 inches wide. Then roll up, sealing the edges as you go. Place the seam side down and fold the ends under so it fits into the pan. (Rough-and-ready method is to push and pat the dough into an oblong larger than the pan. Crease down the middle lengthwise and fold in two. Put in the pan with the seam side down.) Brush the top of the loaf with melted butter. Place the pan on the middle shelf of the oven and cover with a waxed paper or aluminum foil tent. Let the bread rise for 1 hour or until it extends about 2 inches above the pan. Remove from the oven.

Preheat the oven to 425° F (400° F if using a glass pan). Bake for 10 minutes, then reduce the heat to 375° F. Bake another 35 minutes or until golden brown. Remove from the oven and test by thumping on the bottom of the loaf; it should sound hollow. If not, return to the pan and oven for another 5 to 10 minutes.

Remove the bread from the pan and place on a rack to cool. For a soft crust, brush with melted butter.

Yield: 1 large loaf

Tip: I did find a use for my bread machine: If rushed, I use it to do the kneading.

P.D.Q. CHEESE BREAD

Omit lard and stir in 1 cup shredded sharp cheddar cheese with the second addition of flour.

P.D.Q. SWEET BREAD

Add 2 eggs, increase the total amount of sugar to ½ cup, and replace the lard with ½ cup butter, Batter Butter (page 25), or margarine.

P.D.Q. SWEET CINNAMON BREAD

Roll out the sweet dough recipe above, and after the first rising, sprinkle with ¾ cup sugar, 1 teaspoon cinnamon, and ½ cup finely chopped nuts. Drizzle ½ cup melted butter over the mixture, then roll jelly-roll style.

Quickie Buttermilk Bread Loaves

Besides the convenience and speed of this recipe, you'll like the texture and the color. It's a good slicing bread. If you're not avoiding every trace of cholesterol, brush each loaf with butter before baking. Otherwise, brush with buttermilk.

1¾ cups buttermilk

2 tablespoons shortening, chilled

2 tablespoons sugar

2 teaspoons salt

4½ to 5 cups stirred, scooped, and leveled all-purpose flour

2 envelopes (4½ teaspoons) active dry yeast

Herbs, or kosher salt, or poppy, caraway, or sesame seeds
    (optional)

Grease one large baking sheet. Put a large pan of boiling water on the bottom rack of a cold oven.

Combine the buttermilk, shortening, sugar, and salt in a saucepan and place over low heat until the shortening melts. The buttermilk may curdle, but it makes no difference.

In a large bowl of an electric mixer, add 2 cups of the flour and the yeast. Stir together. Add the warm liquids. Mix thoroughly (about 30 seconds) at low speed. Scrap the sides of the bowl. Increase the speed to high and beat for 3 minutes.

If your mixer doesn't have a dough hook, remove the bowl from the mixer and use a wooden spoon or your hands to combine the remaining flour in ½-cup increments.

In a mixer, knead the dough for 6 minutes with a dough hook, or turn out on a floured board or countertop and knead for 8 minutes. The dough should be smooth and elastic.

Cover with waxed paper or a damp tea towel and allow to rest for about 20 minutes. Punch down the dough with your fist and gather together into a ball. Divide the ball into two pieces.

Using a rolling pin, first form a half, then the other half into a 6 x 12-inch rectangle. Roll tightly, jelly-roll fashion, beginning at the longer side. Pinch the ends together tightly. (If you like a tapered loaf, shape gently between your palms.) Place, seam side down, on a greased baking sheet. Cover with waxed paper or aluminum foil and put in the oven to rise for about 25 minutes. Then slash the tops diagonally 3 or 4 times with a single-edged razor blade or sharp knife. Let rise an additional 20 to 30 minutes or until the bread has doubled in size. Remove from the oven.

Before baking, brush the loaves with buttermilk and sprinkle with herbs, kosher salt, or poppy, caraway, or sesame seeds.

Bake in a preheated 400° F oven for 45 minutes or until golden brown. Test by thumping the bottom of one loaf; it should sound hollow. If not, return to the oven for another 10 minutes. Remove from the oven and set onto a wire rack to cool.

Yield: 2 large loaves

Tip: To get two different crusts, brush one loaf with warm water instead of buttermilk after slashing it.

White Soda Bread

Just as some countries have flatbreads and others cornmeal wafers, the Irish have had their soda bread. In cottages throughout the country, peat and turf fires licked at the bottoms of black iron pots. In those pots was a mixture of flour, salt, baking soda, and buttermilk. It might also contain sugar, butter, rolled oats, or whole wheat flour. Raisins too, and dried currants, nuts, or caraway seeds. This is one of the simpler versions, but it's just as delicious.

4 cups stirred, scooped, and leveled all-purpose flour

2 teaspoons baking powder

1 teaspoon baking soda

1 teaspoon salt

¼ cup sugar

1 tablespoon caraway seeds (optional)

¼ teaspoon ground cardamom (optional)

1¾ cups buttermilk (approximate)

For traditional soda bread, you need a covered pan. Grease two 8-inch round layer cake pans or pie plates and use another pair, inverted, as lids. Or use 8-inch round casseroles with lids. Or don't cover at all for a crisper loaf.

Preheat the oven to 375° F (350° F if using glass pans).

In a large bowl combine the flour, baking powder, baking soda, salt, and sugar. If you like a sweeter taste, add cardamom; for a spicier taste add caraway seeds. Mix well. Gradually add enough of the buttermilk to make a soft dough.

Turn out onto a floured surface and knead gently until the dough is smooth and elastic and not sticky, about 3 minutes.

Divide the dough into two parts and shape each into a round loaf. Place each into a pan, patting the dough so that it fits the pan. With a sharp knife or razor blade, cut a 3- to 4-inch long cross, about ½ inch deep, on top of each loaf.

Bake for about 40 minutes or until the loaf is brown and shrinks from the sides of the pan. Test by tapping the loaf on top for a hollow sound. Turn out on a wire rack to cool. The loaves should be cool before cutting.

Yield: 2 large loaves

RAISIN OR CURRANT SODA BREAD

Add 1 to 2 cups seedless raisins or currants with the dry ingredients.

WALNUT-DILL SODA BREAD

Add 2 teaspoons dillweed and 1 cup chopped walnuts to the flour.

LEMON–POPPY SEED SODA BREAD

Add 2 tablespoons each freshly grated lemon zest and poppy seeds.

British-Irish Soda Bread

So named because it is an Irish bread with a British—treacle or molasses—flavoring. This is a much sweeter version of the usual soda bread. It is often baked as a special treat for children, and on holidays, chopped candied fruit or crystallized ginger will be added to really make it extra special.

3 cups stirred, scooped, and leveled all-purpose flour

1 cup whole wheat flour

1 teaspoon salt

1 tablespoon sugar

³⁄₄ teaspoon baking soda

³⁄₄ teaspoon baking powder

¹⁄₂ cup molasses

1 to 1¹⁄₄ cups buttermilk, or more as needed

Grease and flour an 8- or 9-inch round layer cake pan.

Combine the all-purpose flour, whole wheat flour, salt, sugar, baking soda, and baking powder in a large bowl and make a well in the center. Warm the molasses slightly (so that it no longer flows slower than molasses!). Combine with ¹⁄₂ cup of the buttermilk. Add liquid to the flour and stir well. Add more buttermilk as necessary to make a soft dough.

Preheat the oven to 375° F.

Turn the dough out onto a floured surface and knead with well-floured hands only long enough to shape into a ball. Pat out to a circle about 1¹⁄₂ inches thick. Center in a cake pan; if it doesn't fill it, don't worry. Cut a cross in the top of the loaf. Brush the top with more buttermilk.

Bake for 40 to 45 minutes or until the bread is browned and the pan sounds hollow when tapped on the bottom. Cool on a rack and slice thin.

Tip: About that cross: Make it more than ¹⁄₂ inch deep and extend it down the sides of the loaf, essentially quartering the bread. This will enable the bread to rise and bake more evenly.

Whole Wheat "Honey" Bread

An interesting use for Buttermilk "Honey" (page 188). The bread is even better on the second day; it is ideal for sandwiches.

3 cups buttermilk

½ cup honey or buttermilk "honey"

2 tablespoons vegetable oil

4 cups whole wheat flour

1 tablespoon salt

2 envelopes (4½ teaspoons) active dry yeast

4 to 4½ cups stirred, scooped, and leveled all-purpose flour

Grease a 2-quart bowl. Turn on the oven to the lowest setting for 1 minute and no more. *Do not open the door.* You will also need two greased 9 x 5-inch bread pans, preferably shiny metal.

Heat the buttermilk, honey, and oil in a saucepan over low heat until warm. Combine 3 cups of the whole wheat flour, the salt, and yeast in a large bowl of a mixer. Add the warm buttermilk mixture and blend at low speed for 1 minute; increase the speed to medium and beat another 2 minutes. Add the remaining 1 cup whole wheat flour and blend well. With the mixer on low speed, add the all-purpose flour. (Depending on your mixer, you may end up having to stir in most of it by hand.)

Turn out onto a floured surface and knead, adding only as much flour as is necessary to keep the dough from being gluey. After 5 minutes of kneading, the dough should be smooth and elastic. Place the dough in the greased bowl, rotate the dough to grease all surfaces, cover, and let rise in the warm oven for 45 to 60 minutes or until doubled in bulk.

Punch down the dough and divide in half. Shape each half into a loaf (either by continuous tucking under the edges or by rolling it out with a rolling pin and then rerolling jelly-roll style) and place in a greased pan, seam side down. Cover and let the dough rise until the bread fills the pans, 30 to 45 minutes.

Preheat the oven to 375° F (350° F for dull-metal or glass pans). Bake 40 to 45 minutes until the loaf sounds hollow when lightly tapped. Remove from the pan and cool on a wire rack.

Tip: One way to tell that the first rising is complete is to stick two fingers into the dough. If the impressions remain, rising is completed. Don't use the same test with shaped loaves, otherwise you'll have "holey" whole wheat bread.

18 | Judging Buttermilk

Buying buttermilk isn't as simple as one might think.

But then, what is anymore? For example, I was in the dairy department of my supermarket the other day, and there were three different brands of milk, including the store's own Brand A. When I asked the dairy manager the difference between Brand A and the others, he told me that a second brand, Brand B, produces Brand A's gallons and half gallons, while Brand A's quarters and pints are made by Brand C.

This, I discover, is not unusual. Many national and regional milk-producing operations are responsible for supplying dozens of brands, all identical except for the packaging. How can you tell which is which? You can't. However, reading the label will give you a clue. If the milk carton says "distributed by," then it is one of the mass-produced.

Which gives you some idea of the difficulties of trying different brands, and doing so for buttermilk can be even more difficult. First, because you may not have your choice of more than one brand at any one store. Second, because every supermarket in your area may carry the same identical buttermilk but in different packaging. You may have to do some serious looking to find different brands to compare.

I am fortunate. Although my regular market offers but one brand of buttermilk, it is a private label—and it is very good, as my husband's taste buds will avow.

To make buttermilk, whole milk is separated (by gravity or temperature or technology) into skim milk and cream. Skim milk should not be confused with buttermilk, which is still present within the cream. Once the skim has been removed, the full-fat cream is separated into its solid and liquid constituents. The solid is high-fat butter, the liquid is low-fat buttermilk.

Skim milk, by its nature, contains no milk solids, whereas both buttermilk and butter do. Remember melting butter for lobster dipping or popcorn dribbling? Remember how it separates into a clear yellow layer on the top and a thick whitish layer on the bottom? That white layer contains the milk solids. (Any saltiness is unnatural, resulting from salt added to the butter as a preservative.)

In the old days, dairymen relied on nature to get their full-fat milk to separate into skim milk and cream (via cooling and gravity), which took time. Thus all buttermilk was made from soured—but not spoiled—milk.

Modern technology now allows milk to be separated while it is still young and fresh. The butter that results is known as "sweet cream butter," and so is the buttermilk. High quality, *sweet-cream buttermilk* has a clean, sweet flavor very much like good sweet cream. It is not particularly thick but pours like a rich whole milk. It may or may not have flecks of butter granules. It is almost impossible to find except in the dried state. Try your health food store; they may be able to get some for you.

Buttermilk made from sour cream has a slightly sour taste and a buttery aroma. The flavor is clean and pleasant, not at all sour-creamy, and leaves no aftertaste. Again, this is almost impossible to find unless you have a connection with a dairy farmer.

Nor should you really be interested in them except for tasting and drinking. *Sweet-cream* and *sour-cream* buttermilks are uncultured. It is the culturing that is so beneficial to buttermilk. (Think of cultures as similar to starters for bread dough.)

The only way I know to get cultured sweet-cream buttermilk is in its dry state. Which, by the way, is how it is supplied to manufacturers. However, some has been diverted to be sold to consumers. Sounds like a high-tech crime, doesn't it? But it isn't. You'll find dried cultured sweet buttermilk in the dried milk/cocoa section of the supermarket. If your supermarket doesn't carry it, ask for it: SACO. If the manager has never heard of it, tell him/her to call Tony Vanna at 1-800-373-SACO.

Speaking of cultured milk, it is the culturing that has sounded the death knell for good buttermilk.

Instead of culturing sweet-cream buttermilk or sour-cream buttermilk or even low-fat milk (with milk solids added), the dairy industry has found another cheaper, less-tasty-but-who-cares way of making an ersatz buttermilk. It takes plain old skim milk, adds cultures and maybe some butter-flecking to make it look better, then packages it as buttermilk.

The problem is skim milk uncultured and skim milk cultured is still merely skim milk and not buttermilk! Even with flecks of butter added for cosmetic purposes, skim milk does not contain the dissolved vitamins and minerals, the emulsifiers, the lactic acid converted from lactose that is naturally present in real buttermilk.

So the one buttermilk you don't want is cultured buttermilk made from skim milk.

So how do you find the other?

Begin with the labeling on the carton.

What you're looking for is the ingredients portion of the nutritional panel. If it says "cultured from" or "made from skim milk," no good. If it says "made from low-fat milk," that's better. If it says, "made from low-fat milk with whole milk solids," that's still better. If it says "cultured from churned whole milk," that's the best. Unfortunately, you may not in your entire lifetime find a carton that refers to churned milk—unless! Unless you ask the dairy manager of your supermarket to get it for you. Unless you call local dairies and ask them for it. Unless you pester your health food store for it. Unless you put the power of the press behind you by contacting your local food editors. Unless you demand it of the National Dairy Council, the American Dairy Association, or the United Dairy Industry Association. (It doesn't matter which, all three are the same entity. You can reach any and all of them at O'Hare International Center, 10255 West Higgins Road, Suite 900, Rosemont, IL 60018-5616.)

In other words, unless you express your desires, you'll have to take whatever buttermilk the dairy industry thinks you want. However, if you speak up, you'll be surprised at how quickly real buttermilk will reappear on store shelves.

In the meantime, do the best you can and get the best buttermilk available to you according to the label.

The label isn't everything. Your taste buds will tell you more. Unfortunately, your taste for milk may have been ruined by drinking too much pasteurized milk. Pasteurization, which was discovered in 1895, alters flavor. Pasteurized milk tastes cooked. (Dairy professionals divide the taste into "heated," "cooked," and "scorched"—all degrees of caramelization of the milk sugars.) The cooking can even lead to bitterness. Furthermore, pasteurized milk, unlike raw milk, decays. It doesn't sour or ripen, it spoils and rots.

However, if you're only an occasional milk drinker, you probably won't have a problem. The taste of fat and sugar are the baby's earliest tastes. Milk sugar and milk fat (or butter) set our preferences forever. Generally, the more fat in milk or cream or buttermilk, the better it tastes, although people do grow used to skim milk. What there is of aroma in these fresh liquids is mostly associated with fat. The taste of cream is like the taste of the milk it comes from, only moreso. The taste of buttermilk is much the same. So how should a good buttermilk taste versus a bad?

For the answer, I, a non–buttermilk drinker, called in an expert from across the breakfast table.

"Good buttermilk should be rich and of a thick consistency. Tangy with a hint of a bite, but still sweet. Test it with a bit of salt and pepper added, that should bring out the buttery taste.

"Bad buttermilk is thin, watery, wishy-washy, with a slightly sour skim-milk taste. Often it has a hint of a metallic aftertaste. No real tang. Usually no plop-plop consistency."

One thing you can do to improve the taste of whatever buttermilk you buy is to buy your buttermilk—and milk—in cartons. The most common off-flavor in buttermilk (and milk itself) is induced by exposure to light. It's a cabbagy-type taste that develops after 48 hours in milk or buttermilk bottled in translucent plastic and stored in too-well-lit dairy cases. Most milk is now sold in plastic. Buy yours in cartons, and with the latest date stamp possible. One of the benefits of buying good buttermilk is that it has a longer shelf life in your refrigerator than regular milk does. My experience is it will last up to two weeks after the sell date.

But suppose you're like me. You appreciate the virtues and versatility of buttermilk, but you simply can't bring yourself to drink it. How then can you judge it? Just as you do cocoa and vanilla and raw meat and flour and dozens of other products one doesn't normally taste in an uncooked state.

Pour the buttermilk into a measuring cup. Is it thick? A flat grayish-yellow in appearance? Are there butter flecks in the product, which may give it an uneven appearance? (If there aren't, that's okay, too.) If the butter flecks have risen to the surface, that's normal, since they are lighter than the rest of the product.

The no-nos are a thin, runny product . . . smooth in texture and free from curdy particles . . . bluish or bluish-green in color . . . and separated or "wheying-off," which refers to a diluted waterlike layer in the middle or at the bottom or even at the top. It may even appear that the product has been topped off with water.

Take a whiff. One smell and you may be able to tell if the flavor is off: It may smell barny, bitter, cheesy, coarse, flat, green or undeveloped, metallic, yeasty, even rancid.

Unfortunately, the most common off-flavor is high-acid. Take a sip (if you hold your nose, you won't taste it), swish it about your mouth, and do as the professional tasters do: spit it out. If there is a slightly painful sensation on the tongue, there's too much acid. In which case, you'll also notice a lack of pleasing aroma.

The body—before being shaken—should be firm and semi-solid. When you pour it out, it should be smooth as it passes over the lip of the container. There should be no lumps. No gas bubbles or streaks in the curd. No stringing out. If a buttermilk has a rough, coarse body, it may be too curdy. A good test of buttermilk is to pour a small sample into a glass container holding a large proportion of cold water. The individual curds will settle to the bottom where they may be seen. If they are uneven, then this buttermilk is not the best.

What can't be judged is the thickness or viscosity of the buttermilk. Dairy centers have researched the general consumer and found that, like Goldilocks, they prefer their buttermilk not too thick (my husband's an exception) and not too thin. To which the dairy industry shouts, hooray! A thick buttermilk is difficult to handle, and particularly to bottle, although less so when using wax-coated cartons. The industry prefers a thin-bodied buttermilk, which when poured will break, drip, and splash, much like water or skim milk. However, such a watery appearance is too great a contrast with the name of buttermilk; consumers expect differently.

Overall, the product should look uniform and a lustrous white or a white tinged just a bit with yellow, resulting from the presence of butterfat. If too yellow, you should be suspicious. Butter in its natural state is not a "butter yellow," nor should buttermilk be.

Once you've found a buttermilk that you think is good, try cooking with it. If it works, show brand-loyalty but scream like crazy if the dairy changes its formula.

If you can't find one, make your own.

Cook with powdered buttermilk (reconstituted it is not the best-tasting stuff for drinking that my husband has encountered).

Frozen packets of commercial buttermilk cultures are available from dairy and cheese-making supply sources. One packet will innoculate one gallon of milk.

Fresh cultures are available from GEM Cultures, and I can vouch that they make a great buttermilk.

The point is just because the dairy industry makes it difficult for you, don't give up. Buttermilk—good buttermilk—has too much to offer you and your family to quit on it. Remember, thirty years ago, it was almost impossible to buy yogurt. Consumers discovered it, clamored for it, and got it in a plethora of flavors and forms! Yogurt sales multiplied by a factor of 35 in the last twenty-five years.

You can do that for buttermilk, too. And you should—because everything and anything is better with buttermilk!

Index